BUGS

A CLOSE-UP VIEW OF THE
INSECT WORLD

BUGS

A CLOSE-UP VIEW OF THE
INSECT WORLD

By
Chris Maynard

Consultant
David Burnie

A Dorling Kindersley Book

LONDON, NEW YORK, MUNICH
MELBOURNE and DELHI

Project Editor Steve Setford
Project Art Editor Peter Radcliffe
Senior Editor Fran Jones
Senior Art Editor Marcus James
Category Publisher Jayne Parsons
Managing Art Editor Jacquie Gulliver
Picture Researcher Marie Osborn
Production Erica Rosen
DTP Designers Matthew Ibbotson and Louise Paddick

This edition first published in Great Britain in 2005
First published in Great Britain in 2001 by
Dorling Kindersley Limited
80 Strand, London WC2R 0RL

2 4 6 8 10 9 7 5 3 1

Copyright © 2005 Dorling Kindersley Limited

The CIP Catalogue record for this book is
available from the British Library

ISBN 1-4053-1542-3

Reproduced by Colourscan, Singapore
Printed and bound by L.E.G.O., Italy

See our complete
catalogue at
www.dk.com

CONTENTS

INTRODUCTION

Insects, or "bugs" as we like to call them, are the most successful animals on Earth. They've been scuttling around since before the first dinosaurs, and can now be found everywhere from scorching-hot deserts to icy-cold lakes. But insects are very different from us – as different as any alien you've ever seen in films or on television.

To start with, insects don't have a backbone. They also have their skeletons on the outside of their bodies and their flesh on the inside. They don't have lungs, but breathe through holes in their sides called spiracles. What's more, they can taste with their feet and smell with their feelers. Some can even hear through ears on their knees. And so the list goes on...
There are also far more of them than there are of us. Some scientists think that there

MOST INSECTS, INCLUDING THIS LOCUST, HAVE WINGS TO HELP THEM GET AROUND.

may be up to 10 quintillion (10,000,000,000,000,000,000) insects alive at any one time. That's about 1.6 billion insects for every person in the world! Since there's so many of them, perhaps the Earth ought to be renamed "Planet Insect"?

Believe it or not, insects have a tremendous effect on our daily lives. Health experts estimate that one in six people in the world today suffers from an illness transmitted by insects. On the other hand, insects perform such a valuable job in pollinating plants that many of the world's plant species – upon which we rely so much for food – would disappear without them. So, you see, there are plenty of good reasons for learning about these curious creatures.

For those who want to explore the subject in more detail, there are black Log On "bites" that appear throughout the book. These will direct you to some exciting websites where you can find out even more. Welcome to the truly mind-boggling, totally fascinating, and utterly different world of insects!

WHAT ARE BUGS?

We may think we know what bugs are. But most of us find it tricky to say exactly what it is that makes a bug a bug. For a start, bugs are tiny animals that crawl. True. And creep. Correct. And fly into your hair. Not bad. And have zillions of tiny legs. Wrong!

Although many creepy crawlies look like bugs, real bugs only ever have six legs. Anything else is a fake, or a bug that's lost a leg in an accident.

SIX STRONG, JOINTED LEGS, TWO FEELERS, AND A SET OF WINGS PROVE THAT THIS COLOURFUL ASSASSIN BUG IS A GENUINE INSECT.

Bugs or insects

When people use the word "bugs", they usually mean "insects". But strictly speaking "bugs" means something very different to insect scientists (or entomologists, to give them their proper title). This is because among the 30 or so main groups of insects – cockroaches, beetles, ants, flies, and so on – there is a group called "bugs". It has the scientific name of Hemiptera, but all the insects in this group are properly called "true bugs".

WEIRD WORLD

IN 1758, SWEDISH NATURALIST CAROLUS LINNAEUS PUBLISHED DESCRIPTIONS OF 654 SPECIES OF BEETLE. TODAY, WE KNOW OF 370,000 BEETLE SPECIES – AND THE NUMBER'S STILL RISING!

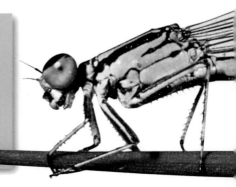

AN EARTHWORM ISN'T AN INSECT.
FOR A START, IT HAS NO LEGS. ITS SOFT,
SLIPPERY, ONE-PIECE BODY ALSO LACKS
FEELERS AND WINGS. BIG OLD WORMS
MAY GROW UP TO 30 CM (12 IN) LONG.

LOG ON...
Check out the bug club
at www.ex.ac.uk/bugclub

True bugs, such as aphids or stinkbugs, have no teeth or mouths that chew. Instead, they have a beak in the shape of a straw with a needle-like point. That doesn't mean they sit around sipping soft drinks all day. What they do is use their beaks to punch holes in things and suck out the juices inside. The "things" they sip from may be plants or animals – even humans if the bugs happen to be bloodthirsty bedbugs.

The leg test

The only sure-fire way to tell an insect from another animal is to count its legs. But first you must persuade it to keep still long enough for you to count. When you're carrying out your leg tests, remember that all insects have six legs. Always!

Many people think that spiders are insects – think again. Check the legs and you'll find that spiders have eight of them, and that proves they aren't insects. Nor are woodlice with 14. Nor are centipedes, which have a minimum of 30 legs (but not 100, as the name

JUST LIKE THIS DAMSELFLY, ALL INSECTS
HAVE THREE-PART BODIES CONSISTING
OF A HEAD, A THORAX (THE MIDDLE BIT),
AND AN ABDOMEN (THE REAR BIT).

implies). The same goes for worms and slugs, which have no legs at all.

Introducing arthropods

The reason why it's so easy to mix up insects and other creeping creatures is because they're all distant cousins. Insects are arthropods. (The "pod" part means we're still talking about legs.) Arthropods all have jointed legs, just as our own legs have knees and ankles. They also have a hard outer skeleton that protects the vital squishy bits inside it. This is known as the exoskeleton. Apart from insects, arthropods include crabs and prawns, spiders, mites, and millipedes.

Luckily, insects differ from other arthropods in a few really important ways. First, they have a body with three parts – a head, a thorax (the middle bit, to which the legs are attached), and an abdomen (the rear bit, which contains the heart, digestive system, and sexual organs). Second, they have a single pair of antennae, or feelers, on their heads. Finally, most insects (but not all) have one or two pairs of wings. Ants and termites, which are definitely insects, don't usually have wings. But most other insects do, and some, including dragonflies and damselflies, can zip along as fast as birds.

The secret of their success

If you get really close to an insect – and remember they're wild animals that might be in the mood to bite you – ponder this question. What is it about insects that makes them the most successful animals ever to have lived on Earth?

THE PRAYING MANTIS USES ITS POWERFUL
MOUTHPARTS LIKE A BUZZ-SAW TO TEAR
PREY TO SHREDS.

The big edge insects have over other animals is their smallness. Most people imagine that your chances in the wild improve if you're big. But bugs hit the big time by being small. The majority of insects are under 25 mm (1 in) long.

Among the smallest even this would seem gigantic. In fact, insects such as fleas, lice, thrips,

BULLDOG ANTS OF AUSTRALIA HAVE LONG, SHARP JAWS LINED WITH SPINES.

and bristletails are so tiny that it's easy to miss them altogether if you blink.

A RAIDING PARTY OF ANTS DRAGS AN UNLUCKY VICTIM BACK TO THE ANT COLONY FOR A BITE TO EAT!

in the tiniest nooks or crannies. Fleas lead a warm and cosy life between the hairs of a cat's fur, and not even the most determined scratching bothers them much. Other insects, like leaf miners and some thrips, live snugly between the paper-thick top and bottom layers of leaves. Beetles of all kinds burrow under tree bark and into the wood, where nobody ever disturbs them. The other really clever thing about being small is that it takes a lot less than a hamburger to feed you. Insects thrive on the tiniest scraps of food. Even in hard times, when other animals struggle to find food, there's always likely to be enough to keep insects happy.

The real minis, like feather-winged beetles, are not much larger than the dot at the end of this sentence. They live happily, if disgustingly, in rotting animal dung, where they snack away on fungus spores. It takes a lot of concentration, and a strong nose, ever to find one.

Smallest of all are the fairy flies. They are about a quarter of the size of a pin-head, but they still get along very nicely, thank you, by laying their eggs in the eggs of other insects.

S mall is smart
Being small means that insects can shelter

WEIRD WORLD
THE BIGGEST INSECTS THE WORLD HAS EVER SEEN WERE DRAGONFLIES THAT LIVED IN SWAMPS ABOUT 300 MILLION YEARS AGO. FOSSILS OF THESE DRAGONFLIES SHOW THAT THEY HAD WINGSPANS OF UP TO 75 CM (29.5 IN).

Small is risky

The most obvious disadvantage of being small is that most other things can squash you flat. As a car windscreen on a summer night shows, millions of insects get flattened every day simply by being in the wrong place at the wrong time. Likewise, if you are an insect minding your own business on a leaf and you're the size of a match-head, a single drop of rain falling on you will feel like being hit by a flying chimney.

The big boys

A few bugs, though not many, have found it easier to get by in the world by growing big. They all live in the tropics, where conditions are kinder to insects and where there is plenty of food all

THE ATLAS MOTHS OF SOUTHEAST ASIA AND INDIA ARE FLYING GIANTS, WITH A WING AREA GREATER THAN ANY OTHER SPECIES OF INSECT.

year round. The heaviest insect is Africa's Goliath beetle. Fully grown, it may weigh 100 grams (3.5 oz) – as much as a cup of sugar. The Hercules beetle is another huge insect, sometimes growing up to 19 cm (7.5 in) long. But because half of its length consists of a massive horn, it actually weighs less than the Goliath. The longest insect

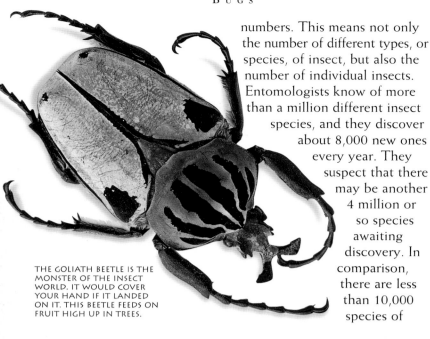

numbers. This means not only the number of different types, or species, of insect, but also the number of individual insects. Entomologists know of more than a million different insect species, and they discover about 8,000 new ones every year. They suspect that there may be another 4 million or so species awaiting discovery. In comparison, there are less than 10,000 species of

THE GOLIATH BEETLE IS THE MONSTER OF THE INSECT WORLD. IT WOULD COVER YOUR HAND IF IT LANDED ON IT. THIS BEETLE FEEDS ON FRUIT HIGH UP IN TREES.

EIGHT OUT OF TEN OF ALL ANIMAL SPECIES ARE INSECTS

of all is the giant stick insect of Indonesia. It can reach 30 cm (12 in), the length of a size-9 shoe. Some tropical butterflies and moths also grow into giants. The wingspan of the Queen Alexandra's birdwing butterfly of Papua New Guinea is 28 cm (11 in), which is about the same width as a large dinner plate.

S trength in numbers
What insects lack in size they more than make up for in sheer

bird in the world and not even a measly 5,000 mammal species.

L ong-term residents
One reason why there are so many insects is that they have been around for an awfully long time. Insects showed up on Earth about 400 million years ago, way before there were mammals,

14

birds, or even any dinosaurs. So they have had plenty of time to find ways to colonize the planet. In fact, the only places you won't find insects are on the tops of the highest mountains, at the North and South Pole, and in the oceans.

Weird food

Another secret of insects' success is their varied diet. You name it – wood, soap, oil, paint, dung – and there's probably an insect that feeds on it. It's a clever tactic. After all, if you can eat your surroundings, you're sure to survive!

IN COLD WINTERS, LADYBIRDS CLUSTER TOGETHER TO HIBERNATE. IN SUMMER, WHEN FOOD IS PLENTIFUL, HUGE LADYBIRD SWARMS MAY FORM.

15

BUGS BY THE BILLION

I f you had a penny for every insect on Earth, you'd be the proud owner of a penny mountain so high that people could ski down it! Scientists know that there are simply too many insects to count. To get an idea of the number of insects crawling around out there, they take samples and study insects closely to see how they live and breed.

Tonnes of termites

Termites are easy to study because they live in colonies and build huge mounds. A large colony may be home to about 7 million termites – as many as the human inhabitants of a city the size of New York, USA, or London, England.

If you could take all the termites in the world and weigh them, and compare the result with the weight of all 6 billion of us human beings, you'd find that termites win convincingly by two to one. That's an awful lot of termites.

Locust swarms

Perhaps the scariest way to get an idea of insect numbers is to stand in the flight path of locusts as they swarm from the desert looking for food. Locusts are a type of large grasshopper. They live in dry areas of north Africa, the Middle East, and Australia. Mostly they are shy, drab-coloured, and lead a pretty lonely life. But when the rains come, they throw some of the biggest, most colourful insect parties ever seen.

Hip hoppers

To prepare for the party, the females lay a lot more eggs than usual in the moist soil. For once, most of the eggs survive. A few weeks later, out hatches an army of young locusts that looks dressed up to go to a ball. Instead of being dull green and grey, these hip-looking hoppers have flashy orange, yellow, and black colours. They are no longer shy, and soon get together to form groups.

Groups join up to form bands, and the bands begin to merge until many square kilometres of desert scrub are heaving with swarms of young hoppers.

LOG ON...
www.insects.org/
has stunning insect photos

Blizzard of bugs

It doesn't take long for the locusts to eat every last leaf and blade of grass. By now they are winged adults, so they fly off to hunt for fresh food. A single square kilometre of countryside may have 200 million locusts moving through it. Really huge plagues can be more than 100 times bigger. The billions of

A SINGLE LOCUST EATS ITS OWN WEIGHT IN GRASS AND LEAVES EVERY DAY. A SWARM OF LOCUSTS CAN STRIP BARE A WHOLE FIELD OF GRAIN IN JUST A COUPLE OF HOURS.

A LOCUST SWARM LOOKS LIKE A BLIZZARD AS IT FILLS THE SKY. THE SWARM KEEPS GOING, FLYING AND FEEDING, UNTIL THE SUPPLY OF FRESH FOOD RUNS OUT.

stretched from Iran in the Middle East to the Atlantic coast of northwest Africa.

locusts in them chomp through as much food in a day as it takes to feed New York City. Wherever the swarm settles, the locusts strip the land bare. In 1957, one outbreak in Africa polished off 167,000 tonnes of grain before it died down. This was enough grain to feed a million people for a year. In 1998, a single plague of locusts kept on growing and spreading until it

Millions of midges

In many parts of the world, clouds of midges swirl above lakes and ponds. Midges are tiny flies – so tiny, in fact, that some people call them "no-see-ums". (Biting kinds ought to be called "boy-can you-feel-ums"!) Midges are far too small to track in the air, but American entomologists

NON-BITING MIDGES LIVE FOR A COUPLE OF WEEKS. THEY MATE ON THE WING IN A SWARM AND LAY THEIR EGGS IN A MASS OF STICKY JELLY ON WATER OR PLANTS.

18

have counted up to 50,000 midge larvae (young) in a single square metre of lake mud. In eastern Africa, by Lake Victoria, midges swarm so thickly that local people gather them in handfuls and press them into mushy cakes. These

can often be seen swarming over garden roses. A female aphid can produce 50 babies a week. If conditions were ideal, and all the young aphids survived and had babies in turn, after just one year the Earth's surface would be

ONE LOCUST SWARM WAS 40 BILLION ADULTS STRONG

midge cakes are then baked on a fire and eaten with great delight. How many midges in a midge cake? No one knows – everybody's too busy eating to count them!

S wimming in aphids
The reason why there are so many insects is no big secret. It's because insects have babies just like beaches have grains of sand. In other words, the numbers are incredible. The champion mother of them all is the aphid. This is a small, soft-bodied insect that feeds on plant sap and

150 km (93 miles) deep in aphids. Thankfully, plenty of animals eat aphids, so we don't have to swim through a sea of them every time we leave the house.

APHIDS ARE GARDEN PESTS. LUCKILY, INSECTS SUCH AS LACEWINGS KEEP APHID NUMBERS IN CHECK – EACH LARVA CAN EAT 200 APHIDS A WEEK.

WHERE INSECTS LIVE

Insects are everywhere. They have colonized our planet more successfully than mammals, birds, or any other type of animal. What's more, they're not averse to sharing our homes with us. And brace yourself for some shocking news, because they also like to take up residence on our bodies – and that's just a bit too close for comfort!

Lice on your head

There's an insect the size of a sesame seed that spends its whole life on humans – the head louse. It latches onto a strand of human hair with its six strong legs and snuggles low, close to the scalp where it's warm and dark. When it gets peckish it crawls down, pokes a hole in the skin, and takes a sip of blood. The only time you'll notice it is when you scratch because itchy louse saliva has dribbled into your

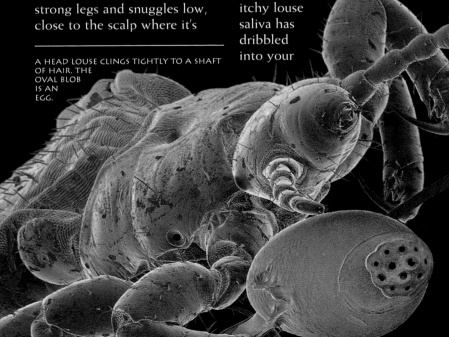

A HEAD LOUSE CLINGS TIGHTLY TO A SHAFT OF HAIR. THE OVAL BLOB IS AN EGG.

A HUNGRY BEDBUG CAN FILL UP
WITH SIX TIMES ITS OWN WEIGHT
IN BLOOD DURING A MEAL.

skin. The little stowaway moved onto your head when your hair brushed against the hair of someone who had lice.

F leas on your pets

Do you have a cat or a dog? If you do, you may well have pets that you didn't know you had. Pets called fleas. And they too suck blood. The good news is that fleas don't live on people the way lice do. They simply come, bite, and go. But they never go far away. They lie patiently in wait in bedding, carpets, and rugs until a meal comes along. Then they pop out and spring onto a passing victim, which could be a cat, a dog, or you – they're not fussy. A hungry flea will bite several times a minute. You'll know your new pet has landed when your skin reacts to the flea bites.

B ugs in the bed

Suppose you got rid of every louse on your head and every flea in your carpets. Time to flop on your bed with a sigh of relief. Well don't! In the cracks of beds and in old mattress seams live other blood-suckers called bedbugs. They emerge at night and ease their sharp beaks into exposed areas of your skin. Then they take a long, thirst-quenching drink. Ten minutes later, and full to bursting, they drop off and stagger away.

WEIRD WORLD

FIREBRATS ARE SMALL, WINGLESS INSECTS KNOWN FOR THEIR ABILITY TO TOUGH IT OUT IN VERY HOT, DRY PLACES. THEY ARE OFTEN FOUND LIVING IN CRACKS BEHIND FIREPLACES OR BAKERS' OVENS.

Roaches in the kitchen

Bitten to pieces, you may take refuge in the kitchen. Guess what? All over the world people share their homes, especially their kitchens, with greasy cockroaches. Roaches feed on any scraps of food and rubbish, from dried pasta to bits of paper. These thumb-size critters can slink under sinks, squeeze through cracks no thicker than a matchstick, and scuttle along pipes to get everywhere. They don't bite or sting, but they do carry germs and reproduce so rapidly that they can take up every corner of your home.

ROACHES HAVE BEEN SEEN ON SPACECRAFT

Here, there, everywhere

Aside from living it up with humans, insects thrive in meadows, scrubland, heaths, woods, and most other habitats. The one habitat they've never really come to terms with is the ocean. A few species skate about over the surface, but apart from that the seas are insect-free. Because the majority of insects feed on plants – and most of the rest prey on these plant-eaters – insects are most plentiful in tropical rainforests, which have the most abundant and varied plant life on Earth. One rainforest tree can be home to about 580 insect species.

DUNG FLIES LIVE IN MEADOWS, WHERE THEY LAY THEIR EGGS IN DUNG PATS. WHEN THE YOUNG HATCH, THEY FEAST ON DUNG.

THIS GRASSHOPPER IS
BRIGHTLY DECORATED TO
HELP IT BLEND IN WITH THE
LEAVES AND COLOURFUL
FLOWERS OF THE RAINFOREST.

They live all over the tree, from its underground roots to its uppermost leaves, and from its gnarled bark right down into the heart of the trunk.

Adapt and prosper

Insects are so widespread because, over millions of years, their bodies have changed, or adapted, to suit a whole variety of surroundings. They are also helped by their amazing exoskeleton. This tough shell is worn on the outside of the body like a suit of armour. It's strong. It's light. It helps to insulate the body. And it's got a waxy waterproof coating that prevents the body fluids from leaking out. Dressed in this protective suit, they can tackle the harshest conditions and live in some of the world's most inhospitable places.

In extreme cold

In which continent is an insect the biggest land animal of all? The answer is Antarctica! The winner is a tiny, wingless midge, a mere 12 mm (0.5 in) long, that survives despite being frozen stiff for much of the year. When the weather warms up, the midge thaws out and becomes active. The only other Antarctic insects are the lice and ticks that live among bird feathers and seal fur. Many insects can survive extreme cold because they have a kind of anti-freeze in their bodies to keep them from

23

freezing solid. It enables rock crawlers, which are cousins of crickets, to live quite happily in mountain snow with not a glove or scarf between them.

In hot and dry places

Insects are also good at living in deserts. Lots of beetles and cockroaches scuttle about in the baking desert heat, digging down into the sand if the sun is too fierce. Many desert insects never see a drop of rain in their lives. But their watertight skeletons prevent their bodies from losing moisture, so they rarely need to drink. The larvae of one African midge dry out completely in long droughts. Although this would kill other animals, when the rain does come the larvae are able to rehydrate, revive, and go about their business.

Under the ground

Some insects have adapted to living in the soil, where there are plenty of roots and rotting plant and animal remains to feast on. Once they take up a life of tunnelling, they have no call anymore for big wings or

THIS DESERT BEETLE GETS THE MOISTURE IT NEEDS BY STANDING STILL AND ALLOWING DROPLETS OF WATER FROM THE EARLY MORNING MIST TO COLLECT ON ITS BODY.

long legs.
That's why
mole
crickets'
wings are
tiny and
tucked out of the way on
their backs. Their short digging
legs are shaped like shovels,
and their bodies are smooth and
round. Ant-loving crickets are
wingless, small, and flat, so they
can wriggle inside an ant colony
and live there without breaking
the place up. They wolf down
ants' eggs, food scraps snatched
from their hosts, and fluids
produced by the ants' bodies.

In the dark

Some insects only visit caves
for food and shelter. Others
move in for good. Many
beetles and crickets love the
damp and dark there and share
it with spiders, millipedes, and
flatworms. Cave crickets have
changed a lot by living as they
do. They never chirp like other
crickets. Their eyesight is
weak, but these crickets make
up for it with hugely long

antennae and legs for smelling
and touching things. Whenever
anything moves nearby, the
crickets detect it immediately.

In many New Zealand caves,
the roof seems to twinkle with
tiny blue stars. The "stars" are
actually fungus gnat larvae that
glow with light to attract prey.
Insects flying towards the
light flutter into sticky
feeding lines lowered by
the fungus gnat larvae.
Then the larvae reel
in their prey and
eat them up.

On water

Many insects love ponds, rivers, and lakes. But they don't all swim or float. In fact, some don't even get wet. This is because insects such as water crickets and pond-skaters are so light that they can stand on top of water. They are held up by a force called surface tension. This force pulls water molecules together and causes the surface of water to behave like a springy skin. The "skin" supports small insects so that they don't sink. They just skate over the surface as if it were ice. As they glide about, they use their front legs to catch food, the middle ones to propel them over the surface, and their back legs to steer.

Under the water

Some insects swim about or crawl along on the bottom of rivers and streams, carrying their own air bubbles with them like tiny scuba divers. Both water boatmen and diving beetles have long, hairy hind legs so they can paddle about underwater. Diving beetles eat insect larvae, snails, and worms. They are excellent swimmers and can even catch small fish and tadpoles. Water scorpions do it differently. They hang just under the surface, breathing air through a snorkel-like tube, ready to grab with their

WHEN HUNTING UNDERWATER, A GREAT DIVING BEETLE BREATHES AIR CARRIED BENEATH ITS WING CASES OR BETWEEN ITS BODY HAIRS.

A WATER BOATMAN TRAPS BUBBLES OF AIR ON THE UNDERSIDE OF ITS BODY, THEN SWIMS ALONG, JUST UNDER THE SURFACE, LOOKING FOR PREY.

strong claws any insects they find resting on the surface.

In odd places

The most bizarre dwelling places belong to insect larvae. The larvae of the petroleum fly live in pools of crude oil, where they wriggle about waiting to devour other insects that get trapped in the sticky goo. Even more strange are scuttlefly larvae. Some have been found living in shoe polish and paint, in dead human bodies pickled in formalin (a fluid doctors use to preserve things), and even in the lungs of living people!

Less gruesome, but still likely to put you off home-made cakes, are the beetle larvae that live in packets of flour in kitchen cupboards. But that takes us back home again, which is where we started.

CADDIS FLY LARVAE LIVE ON THE BOTTOM OF PONDS, HIDING FROM PREDATORS IN A SILK TUBE COVERED WITH LEAVES, STONES, AND SAND.

WEIRD WORLD
THE LARVAE OF CERTAIN FLIES LIKE TO BASK IN THE WATER OF HOT SPRINGS. AT 49°C (120°F), THIS IS THE "OUCH!" END OF WHAT PASSES FOR A SOAK IN A HOT BATH. MOST LIVING THINGS WOULD DIE IF HEATED TO THIS DEGREE.

ON THE MOVE

Forget superheroes! Ignore astronauts! If you really want to find out about flying, you'd better check with the experts – insects. Insects were the first animals on Earth to fly, making their maiden flights more than 300 million years ago. Insects also walk, hop, squirm, and crawl, but it's their wings that make them so special.

DRAGONFLIES CAN HOVER WELL BECAUSE ONE PAIR OF WINGS BEATS UPWARDS WHILE THE OTHER BEATS DOWNWARDS.

B enefits of flight

What's so great about being able to fly? Well, for a start, flying enables insects to wander a whole lot farther in search of food. It also helps them to meet a wider circle of fellow insects when looking for a mate. And if they are in danger of becoming someone's lunch, flight gives them a better chance of escape.

I nsect flying aces

The Formula 1 fliers of the insect world are dragonflies. The fastest reach speeds of more than 50 kmh (30 mph) as they race up and down rivers hunting for bugs to eat. Their flight muscles are so powerful that they can even buzz in one spot like tiny helicopters or fly backwards and loop the loop.

S ize and wingbeats

It sounds like common sense to say that the biggest insects with the most muscles ought to

be able to flap their wings harder and faster than their puny cousins. Well, ignore common sense for once. As a rule, it turns out that the larger the bug, the slower it beats its wings as it flies. Big swallowtail butterflies fly with as few as five beats a second. Medium-size bumblebees drone among flowers at about 200 beats. Meanwhile, some

BUTTERFLIES ZIGZAG FROM SIDE TO SIDE AS THEY FLY, WITH THEIR WINGS MAKING FIGURE-OF-EIGHT MOVEMENTS.

tiny midges, half the size of an eyelash, can beat their wings over 1,000 times a second.

Wing arrangements

Fast fliers, such as damselflies and dragonflies, have two pairs of wings and each set flaps independently. Other insects, including moths and butterflies, have hooks that yoke their pairs of

A COCKCHAFER BEETLE HOLDS ITS THICK WING CASES OUT OF THE WAY TO GIVE ITS REAR WINGS ROOM TO UNFOLD AND FLUTTER.

29

wings together. In flight, both sets move as one. Beetles are slightly more complicated. Although they have four wings, only the rear two are used to get airborne. The front two have developed into tough protective cases. When a beetle is on the ground, these wing cases cover the delicate flying wings behind so that they don't get damaged. When the beetle takes off, the wing cases move up and out of the way while the back pair do all the hard work. This makes beetles slow and clumsy in the air.

How to land on a ceiling

If an insect has just two wings it's sure to be a fly. In true flies, the back wings have become a pair of balancing knobs instead. These help flies to judge their speed and position in the air. What's more, they enable houseflies to pull off the great aerobatic trick of landing upside-down on a ceiling – remarkable, considering that no fly can fly upside-down! As it

MONARCH BUTTERFLIES ARE SERIOUS TRAVELLERS. EACH YEAR THEY FLY SOUTH FROM CANADA TO CALIFORNIA, USA, AND MEXICO TO ESCAPE THE WINTER COLD. THEY COVER UP TO 128 KM (80 MILES) A DAY.

THE BIGGEST FLY IN THE WORLD IS THE SIZE OF YOUR THUMB

scoots along just below the ceiling, a fly lifts its front legs up and grips the surface above. Then it swings its body round, like a gymnast on the parallel bars, and lands four more feet neatly on the ceiling. Plunk, end of trick! Well, not quite…

Sticky feet

As well as this amazing landing ability, flies can also walk quite happily upside down. They can do this because they have sticky pads on their feet. Imagine having Velcro™ on the soles of your feet that was strong enough to take your weight. You would be able to walk anywhere – even on walls and ceilings.

Looking at legs

Insect legs, like human ones, are for walking, running, and jumping. But they seriously put us to shame. If we had legs like insects' we would have to re-write the book of Olympic records. Take grasshoppers and locusts, for example. They have long hind legs with huge muscles, so that when they jump they take off like a rocket. The longest leap by a locust with its wings closed is about 50 cm (20 in) – 10 times the length of its body. (How many of your own body lengths can you jump?) The secret is that, size for size, grasshopper muscles are 1,000 times stronger than human muscles.

FOR THEIR LONGEST LEAPS, GRASSHOPPERS AND LOCUSTS OPEN THEIR WINGS IN MID-LEAP AND GLIDE.

even any breakfast – it can leap 100 times its own height. These great leaping powers come from rubbery pads at the base of its back legs. The pads are squeezed tightly by muscles and kept compressed until the flea needs to jump. Then they are released by a trigger mechanism and the flea is catapulted upwards with an easily heard "click".

FLEAS LIFT OFF 20 TIMES MORE QUICKLY THAN SPACE ROCKETS

High-jump specialist

Insects have got jumping down to a fine art – especially fleas. Well-trained athletes can just about leap up to their own height. In the pole vault they may get up to three times higher. That wouldn't impress a flea. Without any training – or

The mechanics of walking

Not all insects are spectacular jumpers. Walking and running are good enough for most of them. For a long time, nobody could quite figure out how an insect could walk with six legs without tripping over itself. That is, until high-speed film revealed exactly how ants move. As they walked, the ants kept three legs on the ground, and moved the other three legs forwards. And it wasn't just any old three legs. It was always the front and back legs on one side and the middle leg on the other side that stayed put, while the other three legs moved. Then the two sets of legs

Muscles for bustling

Insects get the power to bustle along from muscles inside the thorax – the middle part of the body (this also contains the wing muscles in flying insects). The thorax muscles do the job of moving the legs to and fro, while tiny muscles inside the legs are used to bend the joints.

Sprint challenge

When humans, cats, or horses run fast, there is a point at which all of their legs are in the air at once. Yet no matter how fast insects travel, some of their legs always stay on the ground. Fine, you say. That's because insects don't move

swapped over. If you think about, it's not all that different from the way we walk – 50 per cent of our legs stay down and 50 per cent move forwards!

A HUNGRY FLEA CAN LEAP 30 CM (12 IN) HIGH AND UP TO 600 TIMES AN HOUR.

33

GIANT WATER BUGS PADDLE WITH THEIR REAR AND MIDDLE LEGS. THEY USE THE FRONT PAIR TO SEIZE PREY.

other words, if roaches were as big as humans they'd be able to run 10 times faster than we could!

very fast. Hold on! Let's do some maths to check this. Human beings can run at up to 35 kmh (22 mph). That's about four body lengths a second. A running cockroach, one of the world's fastest insects, has a top speed of about 5 kmh (3 mph). This is only walking speed for us, but for roaches it amounts to 40 body lengths a second. In

All-purpose legs

Insect legs have many more uses than just walking, running, and jumping. Butterflies can use their front pair for tasting food, while bees have special brushes and baskets on their legs for gathering

A PRAYING MANTIS CATCHES VICTIMS WITH ITS FRONT LEGS, WHICH ARE STUDDED WITH SPINES AND HOOKS.

pollen. Grasshoppers can "sing" by rubbing their back legs against their wings to make sounds, and crickets hear using "ears" on their knees.

Legs, you'll remember, can also be used for digging, swimming, and scooting over water. Some insects have even turned their legs into hunting weapons. A praying mantis, for example, has mighty front legs that look as if it's been working out in the gym. It uses them to snatch prey and hold it in a body-lock that stops the victim from struggling as it's eaten alive.

False legs

Caterpillars are tricky. They seem to have zillions of legs, but if you flip one over and count, all you get is six – just like every other insect. The real legs are bunched up at the front. They are used to guide leaves into the caterpillar's jaws and to help with walking. The rest of what look like legs are really muscles that stick out from the body. Each of these "prolegs" has a circle of hairs at the tip. This enables the proleg to grip surfaces as the caterpillar shuffles along.

Some caterpillars don't even bother to walk. To avoid danger, they just drop off their tree-top perch on a silk safety thread!

A SWALLOWTAIL CATERPILLAR GRIPS A PLANT WITH ITS LEGS AND PROLEGS.

HOME MAKERS

Most insects live nomadic lives, flitting from place to place. As long as they can find food, a mate, and shelter, they're content. They're not lazy, it's just that they don't need homes like we do. Some insects take the time to build nests to protect their eggs and young. Still others, called social insects, live together in colonies.

Living together
Social insects include termites, ants, and some wasps and bees. Every colony contains a queen, who lays all the eggs. All the other inhabitants of the colony are her children. Most are workers, who look after the nest, care for the young, and find food. There may also be soldier insects who defend the nest against intruders. They all live together as a one huge family.

Queen of construction
Big families need big homes, and that means lots of building work. Most construction is done by the workers, using their mouthparts. But when a queen common wasp wants to start a new colony, she does all the dirty work herself, as there are no workers to help her. In spring, the queen chews up fibres of wood and turns them into a pulp like papier mâché. This is her building material. First she builds a short stalk, and then adds an umbrella-shaped cap. Below it she builds a comb with half a dozen cells, where she lays her first eggs. While waiting for the

A QUEEN COMMON WASP SHAPES THE WALLS OF THE NEST INTO LAYERS TO PROTECT THE EGGS WITHIN.

eggs to hatch, she builds a series of papery shells around the comb to keep out the wind and rain. When the young wasps turn into adult workers, they carry on the building work to enlarge the nest in time for the next generation. The nest grows swiftly until it's the size of a basketball. When complete, it may hold over 500 wasps at a time. But hard work kills – over spring and summer a total of 10,000 wasps may live there. Most live short lives and soon die of exhaustion.

S olitary wasps and bees

Most wasps and bees live alone, preferring their own company to the hustle and bustle of life in a colony. In fact, they are such loners that they don't even meet the young that hatch from their eggs. Just to show that they care, they make nests for their young in places such as old spider burrows, hollow plant stems, holes in rotting trees, and even in snail shells.

PAPER WASPS FEED PIECES OF CHEWED-UP CATERPILLARS TO LARVAE DEVELOPING INSIDE THE CELLS OF THE NEST.

A MUD-DAUBER WASP BUILDS A MUD NEST ON A TREE AND LAYS A SINGLE EGG INSIDE.

Some wasps and bees are more fussy and put extra effort into nest building. A sand wasp digs a burrow in sandy ground, into which she puts a single egg and a fat caterpillar for her offspring's first meal. She plugs the entrance with sand, head-butts it firmly shut, and flies off.

Masons, potters, carpenters
Sand is just one of the many building materials used by

solitary wasps and bees. Mason bees, and mud-dauber and potter wasps, create mud-pie nests out of balls of moist soil. A female mason bee scouts out a crack in a wall or an old bore-hole in wood left by a beetle. She carries mud to the site and moulds it into a cell, which she lines with chewed leaves and animal hair. Then she packs the cell with pollen and nectar and lays an egg on top. The bee caps the cell with a lid of mud. When she's finished, she leaves behind a nest of half a dozen cells.

You have to like working with wood to be a good carpenter. A female carpenter bee prefers to build with timber rather than mud. To build a nest, she just chews a tunnel into wood. Then she carves out a cell with her jaws where she can lay her egg.

Honey-reared kids

Honeybees that are farmed have a much easier life. In the wild, these social insects build hives in hollow trees or in holes in cliffs. But they are more than

the worker bees collect from flowers. Young bees are first fed on "royal jelly" (a nutritious saliva produced by the workers) and then on honey and pollen.

Ant architects

Ants are ingenious when it comes to nest building. Army ants, for example, have no need

HONEYBEE QUEENS USE SCENT TO CONTROL THE WORKERS

happy to make their homes in the artificial hives that are put out for them by beekeepers. A big hive may have 80,000 workers within, all ruled by a single queen. She will have to lay over 1,000 eggs a day to keep the place buzzing.

The hive itself is filled with several rows of combs. Each comb has hundreds of six-sided cells that are built of wax secreted by the worker bees' bodies. Some cells have eggs and larvae in them. Others are full of pollen and honey, which is made from a sweet liquid called nectar that

BUMBLEBEES LIVE IN SMALL COLONIES. THE QUEENS MAKE THEIR NESTS IN OLD MOUSE BURROWS OR IN CLUMPS OF TALL, THICK GRASS.

several ant-layers thick – very snug!

Wonderful weavers

Just as amazing are weaver ants, which make nests in trees by sewing together groups of large leaves. Teams of workers pull two leaves close to each other and hold them steady. Then smaller workers come along carrying larvae in their jaws. The larvae squirt jets of sticky silk from their heads when touched by the workers' feelers. Their handlers use the silk to "stitch" the leaf edges together.

Underground cities

Ants that live below ground construct complex nests that resemble

WORKER WEAVER ANTS BUILD A TREE NEST. A SINGLE COLONY MAY INHABIT SEVERAL BALL- OR COLUMN-SHAPED NESTS.

for permanent homes, because they are always on the move. Instead, these roving insects make camp in a temporary nest formed from their own bodies! They cluster together on the forest floor and grip each other with their clawed feet. The finished nest (called a "bivouac") is like a closed bag,

WEIRD WORLD

AN ANT SUPERCOLONY WAS FOUND IN JAPAN. IT CONTAINED MORE THAN 300 MILLION WORKERS LIVING IN 45,000 LINKED NESTS.

A PROCESSION OF LEAF-CUTTER ANTS CARRIES BITS OF VEGETATION BACK TO THE NEST TO FERTILIZE THEIR FUNGUS GARDEN.

LOG ON...
www.nhm.ac.uk/nature-
online/life/insects-spiders/

miniature cities. After a queen ant has mated, she hunts for a crack in the soil and digs a little chamber. Here she lays her first batch of eggs and guards them until they hatch.

When the first worker ants emerge, the new colony gets seriously busy. The worker ants turn the area into a building site as they dig down to create a maze of tunnels and chambers.

The main chamber belongs to the egg-laying queen. Around this are chambers for the rest of the colony. Some just have eggs in them, others contain larvae, and a third type holds only pupae. Workers move the young between the different chambers as they grow.

S ubterranean gardens

Leaf-cutter ants are great gardeners! It may sound odd, but these ants actually grow their own food – fungus. The ants tend

from chewed-up leaves mixed with ant dung. When a queen leaves to found a new nest, she carries a tiny piece of fungus with her to start a new fungus garden.

A nt heap

Some ant colonies create mounds on top of their nests. Most spectacular are the piles of

fungus gardens in their underground nests. They grow the fungus on a fertilizer made

pine needles that wood ants stack up. For a big colony of 100,000 ants the pile, which looks like a thatched roof, may be waist high. Wood ants prey on other insects, and a single colony may hunt down thousands of victims each day.

Two rulers

Only termite colonies have both a queen and king. The queen lays the eggs, and the king fertilizes them. (In social wasps, ants, and bees, the male who fertilizes the queen's eggs dies before the colony is founded.) Day and night, for most of her long life, the queen lays an egg every few seconds. In becoming a full-time egg factory, she swells up like a fat, white sausage. Too big to move, she relies entirely on the workers to feed and care for her.

Termite mounds

The tallest of all insect structures are termite mounds. The nests of African termites often reach a height of 7.5 m (25 ft). The human equivalent

THIS STRANGE MOUND WAS BUILT BY A SPECIES OF AFRICAN TERMITE. THE WEIRD, UMBRELLA-SHAPED CAPS MAY PROTECT THE NEST AGAINST TORRENTIAL RAINSTORMS.

TENDED BY WORKERS, A BLOATED TERMITE QUEEN MAY LAY 30,000 EGGS PER DAY. THE BIG TERMITE IN FRONT OF HER IS THE KING.

of this would be building a skyscraper 9.6 km (6 miles) high! Each towering mound is made from pellets of soil mixed with termite saliva. It's quite a feat, especially when you consider that worker termites are blind!

A termite tower works like an air-conditioning unit. It sucks hot air from the nest below and allows cooler air from above to replace it. This prevents the termites from roasting in the heat created by millions of bustling bodies.

Under the tower sits the nest itself, which is up to 3 m (10 ft) across. It contains a den for the queen, nurseries for the larvae, and fungus gardens. Leading from the nest and up through the tower are branching tunnels. The workers widen or narrow the tunnels to adjust the speed of air flowing through the nest. This ensures that the temperature in the nest never varies by more than one degree.

SOLDIER TERMITES PROTECT THE TERMITE NEST FROM ATTACKERS.

PROUD PARENTS

By human standards, insects are poor parents – most abandon their eggs as soon as they're laid, so the young must fend for themselves. The one thing they are good at is having vast numbers of children. But insects setting out to start a big family need a special ingredient – romance!

Attracting a mate

When women and men want to be attractive, they wear perfume or aftershave. A similar thing happens in the insect world. Butterflies and moths are the real wizards of scent. Some male butterflies find partners by flying past a female and scattering sweet-smelling dust onto her. (Sweet smelling to another butterfly, that is.) The scent is so magical that the star-struck female lands and sits still, inviting the male to mate with her.

With moths, it's the females who give off romantic smells. A female emperor moth's scent is so bewitching that even a male emperor flying along minding his own business several kilometres away can't resist. As soon as his antennae pick up traces of her perfume in the air, he zigzags off at full speed to track down the wearer and declare his romantic intentions.

BUTTERFLIES AND MOTHS USE THEIR ANTENNAE TO DETECT SMELLS. SOME MALE MOTHS CAN SMELL A FEMALE MORE THAN 11 KM (6.75 MILES) AWAY.

WHEN A MALE CICADA SINGS, THE RAPID CLICKS HE MAKES ON HIS SOUND ORGANS ARE AMPLIFIED BY AIR SACS IN HIS BODY. THE RESULT IS A LOUD WHINING NOISE.

Love songs

When crickets chirp or cicadas sing, what they are up to is the insect version of serenading under a balcony. And the louder they chirp, the dreamier they sound to any would-be mate within hearing. A male cicada can belt out a song with the power of 100 decibels – that's louder than a vacuum cleaner going full blast! He "sings" by clicking away at incredible speed using drum-like organs called tymbals on either side of his abdomen.

The light of love

Fireflies are really beetles. They get their name because the males look for mates by flying through the night sky flashing lights from their abdomens. Keen females flash back to signal their acceptance. The lights are made by chemicals inside the fireflies' bodies.

Mating marathon

Once their courtship is over insects can mate. Most mating insects like to get things over quickly. But dragonflies and damselflies remain locked in a passionate embrace for up to 10 hours! They also perform some weird acrobatics. When an amorous male finds a willing female, he loops his abdomen around to

MATING DAMSELFLIES JOIN TO FORM A HEART SHAPE, WITH THE MALE (RIGHT) GRIPPING THE FEMALE'S NECK AND HER TAIL BENDING FORWARDS.

45

A STINKBUG GUARDS HER EGGS, WHICH SHE HAS GLUED TO A PLANT STEM.

pouch on his abdomen using the tip of her tail.

Dangerous lunch date

When a male praying mantis goes courting, predators are the least of his worries. If he's not careful, he may end up being eaten for lunch by his lover! The female is larger than the male, and well known for biting off her suitor's head and devouring his body.

To try to escape this bizarre fate, the male moves towards her very cautiously. He waves his antennae, stamps his feet, and waggles his body to show his intentions are honourable. When he's close (but not too close), he leaps onto her back and out of reach of her spine-studded front legs. If he's successful, he can then mate without being eaten alive.

Throw-away eggs

Once insects have mated, their next job is to find places to lay their eggs. Many appear to have a careless attitude about it.

get a grip on her neck. The couple flies off together with the female in a firm neck-lock. After a while they land. Then she curls her long body between her legs to collect sperm from a

46

A BLUEBOTTLE GETS ITS NAME FROM ITS METALLIC BLUE ABDOMEN. THIS ONE IS LAYING HER EGGS ON SOME ROTTING MEAT.

With a few twitches of her abdomen, a female stick insect sprinkles her eggs around like confetti. It looks as if she doesn't give a hoot about the tiny eggs. But by scattering them widely, she makes it very difficult for predators to find them.

Eggs in hiding

All insects try to place their eggs where there's plenty of food and shelter nearby. That's why a bluebottle fly likes to lay eggs on a decaying corpse. A dead mouse or bird provides a mountain of meat for the fly's maggots when they hatch.

An acorn-eating weevil takes a lot of time to give its eggs a good start in life. It drills a hole into a fresh acorn with its snout, then turns around and injects an egg into the bottom of the hole. The

THE HOUSEHOLD COCKROACH KEEPS ITS EGGS IN A SPECIAL CASE. THE EGG CASE HANGS FROM HER REAR, AND SHE LUGS IT AROUND UNTIL THE EGGS HATCH.

47

ALTHOUGH DESERTED BY THEIR PARENTS, THESE BEETLE LARVAE ARE COVERED IN HARD SPINES TO PROTECT THEM.

young weevil grub hatches out and – oh joy – finds itself living inside its own dinner!

Other insects take great care to hide their eggs so they won't be stolen. Some species of water bug are just as good at this as Easter Bunnies. They stash their eggs away so carefully in the stems of water plants that they are invisible to any would-be egg stealers.

Egg heroes

A few insects never leave their eggs at all. They do their best to defend them from any creatures with an eggs-for-lunch gleam in the eye. One example is a tiny thrips that feeds on fungus and lives in the rainforests of Panama. (Thrips are slender insects with two pairs of narrow, hair-fringed wings.) The female thrips not only protects her eggs, but also stays with them after they have hatched. During the day she

sites, and in the evening she devotedly herds them back to safety under the bark of a tree.

Although most insect fathers rarely hang around to help with the childcare, there are a few

APHIDS BEAR LIVE YOUNG AND REPRODUCE WITHOUT MATING

S uper mum

A mother earwig digs a small hole in the soil under stones and lays 20 to 50 pearl-white eggs in it. While she waits for them to hatch, she turns them regularly and cleans off dirt and harmful fungus. If a predator comes too close, she threatens the intruder by fiercely waving her sharp pincers at it.

After the eggs hatch she stays at the nest and feeds her young by vomiting up food from her stomach. Baby earwigs usually stay with their mother for a week or so until they can fend for themselves. But if home proves too cosy and they don't want to leave, mum has a good way of persuading them to move out – she tries to eat them!

exceptions. The male giant water bug allows the female to glue batches of eggs onto his back. The eggs stay attached to dad until they hatch. He carries them around and strokes them to keep them clean. It's a tough job, because the eggs slow him

TO REPEL ATTACKERS WHO TRY TO REACH HER YOUNG, A FEMALE STINKBUG GIVES OFF A POWERFUL, VILE-SMELLING SCENT.

A BUTTERFLY STEPS OUT OF THE
PUPA IN WHICH IT CHANGED
FROM A LONG, LOOPING
CATERPILLAR INTO A
STYLISH-LOOKING
ADULT.

down so much that he
can't even feed while he
is hauling them around.

Fight for survival

Insect parents need to produce
lots of young to ensure that
some survive to become adults
and carry on the family line.
(Young insects make nutritious
snacks for birds, frogs, and a
whole range of other animals.)
    Young froghopper bugs have
found that one of the
best ways to avoid
being gobbled
up is to
stay out of sight.
The froghoppers
blow a frothy liquid out of their
rear as they feed on plant sap.
Soon they are entirely covered
in foam and hidden from view.
We call this foam "cuckoo spit".

Growing up

As a young insect grows from
egg to adult, it sheds its skin
    several times to produce a

larger exoskeleton. Insects such as cockroaches, crickets, true bugs, earwigs, and damselflies, are all born looking pretty much like their parents. We say they go through "incomplete metamorphosis" in order to become adults. This is a long-winded way of explaining that they don't change very much as they shed their skins and get bigger. Mostly they just sprout a set of wings and get larger appetites. About one in ten of all insects develops in this way.

Big change
Nine out of ten new-born insects become adults by going through "complete metamorphosis". This means that they change dramatically as they grow up. The larva that hatches from the egg looks no more like its mum and dad than a worm resembles a hedgehog. When it gets to the right size, the larva sheds its skin for the last time. The new skin hardens into a protective shell called a chrysalis. (Some insects spin a silken bag, or cocoon, around the chrysalis.) In this state, called a pupa, it rests quietly while its old body breaks down and a new, adult body is built.

AS A DAMSELFLY SHEDS ITS SKIN FOR THE LAST TIME, IT PUMPS BLOOD INTO ITS NEWLY FORMED WINGS TO EXPAND THEM TO THEIR FULL SIZE.

It emerges from the pupa looking completely different.

Insects that undergo this larva–pupa–adult change of life include beetles, flies, ants, bees, wasps, moths, and butterflies.

A YOUNG FROGHOPPER'S FROTHY COAT STOPS ITS SOFT BODY FROM DRYING OUT.

GOOD SENSE

I nsects don't have much in the brain department. An insect brain contains anything from a few thousand brain cells to just over a million, depending on the species. Humans, by contrast, have hundreds of billions of brain cells. However, insects make up for their tiny thoughts by having unbelievably good senses.

Enormous eyes

As much as 80 per cent of an insect's brain is devoted to processing information from its eyes and antennae. That may sound like a lot, but it's understandable when you consider the size of some insect's eyes. A dragonfly's eyes, for example, take up most of the space on its head, just like hair does on your own. In fact, dragonfly eyes are so big

WITH HUGE EYES THAT WRAP RIGHT ROUND ITS HEAD, A DRAGONFLY HAS NEARLY ALL-ROUND VISION.

A COMMON WASP HAS THREE SIMPLE EYES ON TOP OF ITS HEAD AND A BIG, BULGING COMPOUND EYE ON EACH SIDE.

SIMPLE EYE

COMPOUND EYE

and bulgy that they almost meet at the top of the head.

This enables a dragonfly perched on a reed to peer up, down, ahead, and behind without ever having to move its head. It's a great trick, and it helps dragonflies to be ruthless hunters of other insects.

In fact, dragonflies' eyesight is so good that they can still catch mosquitoes at dusk, when our own eyes wouldn't be able to see a thing in the gloom.

Extra eyes

Humans have two eyes, both pretty much the same. Insects can have four, five, or even more eyes dotted about their heads, and they are not at all alike. The smallest of them are known as simple eyes, which consist of a layer of light-sensitive cells. Simple eyes can tell the difference between light and shade, but they can't form images. That job is left to the larger eyes, which are called compound eyes. Each compound eye is packed with hundreds, or even thousands, of tiny lenses – nearly 30,000 in the case of some dragonflies. We do not know exactly what insects see with their compound eyes, but

WEIRD WORLD

SOME NOCTURNAL INSECTS CAN DETECT A LIGHT SOURCE EVEN WHEN THEIR EYES HAVE BEEN COVERED UP. THIS IS BECAUSE THEY ALSO HAVE TINY LIGHT-SENSORS DOTTED OVER THE SURFACE OF THEIR BODIES.

we do know that they are incredibly good at detecting movement – which is one reason why insects tend to be so difficult to catch!

Although insect larvae usually only have simple eyes, most adults have compound eyes as

ITS LEG BASKETS BULGING WITH POLLEN, A HONEYBEE USES ITS ULTRAVIOLET VISION TO HOME IN ON ANOTHER FLOWER.

well. A wasp, for example, has three simple eyes arranged in a triangle on top of its head, and a compound eye on either side. The simple eyes may help the wasp to balance as it flies about.

Supervision

Insect eyes can see things that are invisible to humans. One of the things they can see is ultraviolet light – the part of the Sun's light that can give people sunburn. Many flowers have patterns of lines that show up in ultraviolet light. The lines,

WEIRD WORLD

A WORKER HONEYBEE PERFORMS A SPECIAL DANCE TO TELL OTHER BEES WHERE TO FIND FOOD. THE WATCHING BEES ALSO SAMPLE FLOWER SCENTS ON ITS BODY AND NECTAR THAT IT SICKS UP.

LOG ON...
www.insecta.com
has a "bug of the month"

THESE TWO WORKER ANTS ARE COMMUNICATING BY TOUCHING FEELERS. THEY EXCHANGE SCENTS THAT ACT LIKE CHEMICAL MESSAGES.

Insects smell with their antennae, which are covered in tiny, scent-detecting hairs. Because antennae are also used for touch (which is why we often call them "feelers"), it's probably a bit like being able to smell the world with your fingertips.

which are called honey guides, lead insects to the flowers' nectar. Insects can see honey guides in broad daylight. The honey guides help the insects to make a "bee-line" for the food. Humans can see honey guides only if all the other colours in daylight are kept out – something that only happens in the laboratory.

A nt communication

When two ants meet, the first thing they do is to stroke one another's antennae to feel and smell what the other ant has to say. As the feelers brush, they swap scents that are messages about food, eggs, danger, and other gossip to do with

F eels smelly

Don't be fooled into thinking that all insects have good eyesight. Ants' eyes are very weak – in fact, many ants are blind. Yet they get around with no problem at all because they have a terrific sense of smell. But when we're talking of smell in the insect world, we're not talking about noses.

LONGHORN BEETLES HAVE SMALL EYES BUT LONG ANTENNAE UP TO FOUR TIMES THE LENGTH OF THEIR BODIES.

55

the ant colony. One scent could be a message that means "Let's carry that dead ant out of the nest." Another scent might be a rallying cry that says "Call up the troops to defend the nest!" Yet another could be a warning signal to tell everyone to flee from danger.

A similar thing happens in a beehive. When a honeybee is attacked or injured, it gives off a special scent. Other bees smell it and react as if an alarm bell has rung. They buzz about angrily and get ready to sting anything nearby that looks like it is going to attack the hive.

Taste detectors

If smelling with your fingertips sounds odd, how about tasting with your feet? This is what insects can do, because they have special taste-detecting hairs on their feet as well as on their mouthparts.

What use is that? Well, let's look at the cabbage white butterfly. A female cabbage white prefers to lay her eggs on cabbages, because they are the favourite food of her fussy larvae. She can tell cabbages apart from other plants by the taste of the mustard oil that their leaves give off. When she lands on a leaf, she just has to stamp up and down to find out if it's the right kind of plant to lay eggs on.

WITH BIG COMPOUND EYES AND BRISTLING WITH SENSE HAIRS, FLIES ARE WELL-EQUIPPED TO MAKE OUT THE WORLD AROUND THEM.

WHEN SOME MOTHS HEAR A BAT, THEY
FOLD UP THEIR WINGS AND PLUMMET TO
THE GROUND TO AVOID BEING EATEN.

Touch and movement

As well as sense hairs for smelling and tasting, insects also have tiny hairs on their bodies that are sensitive to touch and which can detect vibrations in the air. When these hairs are bent – by an object or moving air – they send nerve signals to the insect's brain.

By detecting vibrations in the air caused by the movement of other animals, an insect can tell if an attacker is approaching or its prey running away.

caused by landing too hard after a long jump, it's actually an ear, and it's used to listen out for the mating songs of other crickets.

Having ears in weird places is common among insects. In praying mantises, the ears are on the thorax, while lacewings and some moths have theirs on the wings. The ears of cicadas,

SOME FLIES CAN SMELL ROTTING FLESH SEVERAL KILOMETRES AWAY

Listen up

Like us, insects are able to hear sounds, but they don't have an ear sticking out from each side of the head. Crickets have a big swelling below the knees of each front leg. Although the swelling looks like a bump

grasshoppers, and other moths are on the abdomens.

Some moths can use their ears to eavesdrop on the high-pitched sounds that hunting bats make. If they are lucky, it gives the moths time to dodge out of the way and escape.

SHAPE AND COLOUR

Like spies in disguise, insects go to great lengths not to be caught. The best way to avoid ending up in the belly of a predator is to stay out of sight. By adapting their shape and colour, insects have developed some cunning tricks to escape the gaze of sharp-eyed hunters.

Concealed by camouflage

Using colour and shape to blend in with the surroundings is called camouflage. It can be very simple, such as the way a green grasshopper is hidden among plants by its green colour. But some insects have turned camouflage into an art form. Their fantastic colour patterns and weird shapes enable them to become pretty much invisible against particular backgrounds.

THE GIANT LEAF INSECT LOOKS LIKE A SLIGHTLY SHRIVELLED LEAF, COMPLETE WITH HOLES.

A MERVEILLE DU JOUR MOTH IS EASY TO SPOT ON TREE BARK, BUT IT DISAPPEARS AGAINST A BACKGROUND OF LICHEN.

Lichen lovers

Lots of insects have discovered that tree-trunks make great places to hide. Some Central American flatid bugs have see-through bodies. When they rest on tree bark, a predator sees the bark underneath, not the bug itself. Many beetles and moths lie low on lichen – a papery, fungus-like stuff that grows on tree-trunks. Their mottled markings perfectly match the lichen's brown and white colours, so they melt away from view.

Leaves and sticks

Leaf insects have flattened abdomens and leg segments that give them a remarkable

look just like a normal twig. Most camouflage works on the principle that if you stay still, you won't be spotted. But on a breezy day, with trees and bushes swaying, standing dead still might give you away.

So, the stick insect rocks its body gently to and fro, like a twig blowing in the wind.

Thorn bugs

Another type of camouflage is to dress up as something inedible. That's what some treehopper bugs do. They have a pointed extension to the thorax that makes them the spitting image of thorns. These "thorn bugs", as they are also known, cluster on plants, where they feed on plant sap, happy in the knowledge that they are of no interest to hungry birds. After all, who'd want to eat thorns? The only time that the bugs move is to find a new feeding spot.

resemblance to leaves. Their markings imitate the ribs and veins of leaves, while the edges of the body may be brown and crisp, like a dying leaf. The excellent disguise conceals them from predators, but there's always a small risk that they might end up getting munched by a plant-eater by mistake!

As it sits contentedly in a tree or bush, a stick insect's long, slender body and legs make it

Warning colours

Some insects don't care two hoots if hunters know where they are. They go out of their way to be seen by having bold markings and snazzy colours. They seem to be saying, "Hey, over here! It's me!" That's because they are either loaded with poison or pack such a powerful sting or passionflower vines. It sounds romantic, but it doesn't make the caterpillars sweet to eat. The leaves are rich in cyanide, and this deadly poison ends up stored in the caterpillars' spiky

ONE GRASSHOPPER LOOKS JUST LIKE A LUMP OF QUARTZITE ROCK

bite that few animals ever dare to tangle with them. Orange, black, yellow, and red are often used to warn other animals to steer clear of an insect.

P oisonous postman
Postman caterpillars
feed on the
leaves of

THE POSTMAN CATERPILLAR'S POISONOUS SPIKES HELP TO DETER BIRDS FROM ATTACKING.

bodies. The brightly decorated postman caterpillars go around with an "eat me and drop dead" attitude. It's good advertising, and it gets noticed – birds never touch them more than once!

Insect mimics

Lots of harmless insects have taken to copying the looks of insects that sting or contain vile-tasting chemicals. It's a clever way of enjoying the bad reputation of another insect without the hard work! These copycats are called mimics. Hoverflies, for example, are wasp and bumblebee mimics. They look and hover like wasps and bumblebees, so few animals attack them for fear of getting stung.

Not all mimics copy insects. One weevil in New Guinea has discovered that life is a lot safer if it acts like a spider. Although

HOVERFLY   WASP

THIS HOVERFLY (LEFT) IS ABOUT THE SAME COLOUR, SIZE, AND SHAPE AS A COMMON WASP (RIGHT). HOWEVER, THE HOVERFLY HAS TWO WINGS AND THE WASP FOUR.

THE WINGS OF THIS BANANA-EATING
BUTTERFLY FROM NEW GUINEA CARRY
LARGE EYESPOTS FOR STARTLING PREDATORS.

it has six legs to a spider's eight, it still runs about like a spider and holds its legs in a spidery way. This simple trick improves its chances of surviving.

S hock tactics

Sometimes it's better to hot-foot it out of tricky situations, rather than to sit still and hope that you're not seen. To aid their escape, some insects have a large eye-shaped spot on each wing. If disturbed, they spread their wings and flash these eyespots. The startled attacker thinks it has picked on a larger animal than it bargained for. The insect wins a split-second chance to make its getaway.

A ct menacing

Predators can often be deterred if their potential prey puts on a menacing display.

The puss moth caterpillar has a red ring and black eyespots at the front of its thorax. When threatened, it pulls its head back into its thorax, creating a hideous, face-like pattern. If a bird sees it rearing up and swaying menacingly like an angry snake, it backs off and the caterpillar survives to see another day.

THE PUSS MOTH CATERPILLAR LASHES ITS
WHIP-LIKE "TAILS" TO AND FRO TO MAKE
ATTACKERS THINK THEY ARE STINGS.

FEEDING FRENZY

Why is a group of hungry kids like a swarm of locusts? The answer is that both can empty a fridge in less than a minute! The kids, we hope, would be polite enough to use knives and forks when they eat. Since bugs don't care for cutlery, they have a range of mouthparts to get food into their bellies.

Two pairs of jaws

The shape of an insect's mouthparts depends entirely on its eating habits. Insects that chew their food – including beetles, grasshoppers, and termites – have a pair of jaws called mandibles. The jaws have serrated edges, rather like the teeth of a saw. These powerful tools move sideways to cut and grind up hunks of food. Behind the mandibles lie a second pair of jaws, called maxillae, which are not quite as powerful. The maxillae are mostly used to line up the food ready to push it on its way into the insect's abdomen. But why bother to give yourself jaw-ache

AFTER THESE HORSEFLIES HAVE GORGED THEMSELVES ON BLOOD, THEY WILL FLY OFF LEAVING PAINFUL WOUNDS BEHIND.

chewing when you can suck, sip, or slurp up your food instead...

B lood-suckers

Lots of insects like to take their meals the easy way – as a drink. Animal blood is a nourishing, protein-filled food drunk by horseflies and other blood-sucking insects. Once a female horsefly finds an animal, she chases after it. When she lands, she slashes open the skin with her curved, sword-like jaws. Next she uses a sharp rod to drill up and down to get the blood flowing. As she sucks the blood up through her mouth tube, she pumps saliva into the wound to prevent the blood from clotting.

What's the male horsefly doing while this bloodthirsty business is going on? Probably sitting on a flower somewhere drinking nectar, because it's only the females that have biting mouthparts and feed on blood.

N ectar sippers

Moths and butterflies carry a long tongue (known as a proboscis) rolled up like a length of fire hose under the head. After they land on a flower, muscles in the head start to pump blood into the tongue. It uncoils and reaches down into the base of the flower where the sugary nectar is stored. Then the butterfly takes a dainty sip.

BUTTERFLIES HAVE NO JAWS, JUST A TUBE-LIKE TONGUE THAT STAYS COILED UP WHEN NOT IN USE.

Sap slurpers

True bugs have mouths shaped like the needles doctors use for injections. Many, including cicadas, treehoppers, and aphids, use this little syringe to punch a hole in a plant so they can drink the mineral-rich sap inside. Aphids tap the veins of plants where the sap flows

YOU CAN CLEARLY SEE BOTH THE JAWS AND THE SUCKING MOUTHPARTS OF THESE DRINKING BEES.

strongest. In fact, the sap flows so powerfully that the aphids hardly have to slurp at all. They glug down so much that sap spouts out of their rear end as honeydew. This is the sweet syrup that ants adore.

Liquidize your enemies

Some insects that enjoy liquid lunches are ruthless killers. The robberfly snatches other insects in mid-air with ease. From its perch on a rock or a twig, the robberfly rockets upwards, grabs a flying insect with its spiny feet, and lands for the feast. Its mouth stabs into the victim's body and injects saliva, which quickly dissolves the innards. After sucking out the mushy liquid, it takes

A BRAZILIAN SHIELD BUG DRINKS SAP FROM A PLANT STEM. SOME SAP SLURPERS, SUCH AS APHIDS, CAN PASS HARMFUL VIRUSES BETWEEN PLANTS AS THEY FEED.

nest construction and to handle building materials, while their tube-like proboscis is normally used to feed on nectar. But some hunting wasps use their jaws to squeeze the body fluids from their victims, which they then suck up.

off, leaving behind the lifeless, shrivelled body of its prey.

Dual-purpose mouths
Wasps and bees have both biting and sucking mouthparts. The biting jaws are used for

A ROBBERFLY STABS ITS VICTIM BETWEEN THE HEAD AND THORAX. DEATH IS ALMOST INSTANT.

CLUTCHING A TWIG WITH ITS PROLEGS, AN OAK SILKMOTH CATERPILLAR MAKES SHORT WORK OF ANOTHER LEAF. ITS JAWS WORK FROM SIDE TO SIDE AS IT CHEWS THROUGH THE LEAVES AND STEMS OF OAK TREES.

WEIRD WORLD

THE LONGEST INSECT TONGUE IN THE WORLD BELONGS TO DARWIN'S HAWKMOTH OF MADAGASCAR. MEASURING 28 CM (11 IN) TO THE TIP, IT IS USED TO SIP NECTAR FROM THE DEEP FLOWER TUBES OF STAR ORCHIDS.

S pit soup

Houseflies probably have the most disgusting eating habits of all insects. When a fly lands on something good (it can tell the flavour using taste buds on its feet), it says "yum" to itself and promptly vomits all over it! The fly's saliva digests the food and turns it into a soupy liquid. The fly mops it all up with the spongy pad at the end of its mouth tube. So, next time a cute little fly appears to kiss a piece of food, remember what it's really doing!

L eaf crunchers

A liquid diet isn't to the taste of all insects. Many prefer solid food such as crunchy leaves. The chief leaf-eaters are grasshoppers, leaf beetles, katydids, and the caterpillars of butterflies and moths. Caterpillars are often called "feeding machines", because they have to eat continually while they are larvae, so they can store up enough proteins in their bodies for egg-laying as adults. Their mouthparts are perfect for making mincemeat out of leaves. The jaws have overlapping edges that slice up leaves like scissors and grinding plates to mash every mouthful to a pulp.

Digestive aids

You may not think wood very appetizing, but it's perfect for meeting the daily needs of insects such as wood termites and wood-boring beetles. Most animals can't digest cellulose, which is one of the main ingredients of wood. But these insects can survive on a diet of wood because they have microbes (tiny, single-celled organisms called protozoa and bacteria) living in their digestive systems. In return for a cosy home in an insect's belly, the microbes make chemicals called enzymes, which break down the cellulose into much simpler substances that the insect can digest.

Meat-eaters

Some insects, including ground beetles, mantises, and many ants, enjoy nothing better than to tuck into a chunk of fresh meat. The fiercest and fastest of all ground beetles is the tiger beetle. Like every other meat-eating beetle, it has two sets of jaws – a set of big jaws for chopping up victims and a set of smaller ones for stuffing

THE TIGER BEETLE HAS SHARP EYESIGHT. IT CHASES PREY BY SPRINTING ON ITS LONG LEGS AND MAKING SHORT FLIGHTS WITH ITS WINGS.

and pulled to death. Small victims may be dragged back to the nest by individual ants. But larger prey may require a team of workers to chop it up into more manageable pieces.

S weet tooth

Ants adore sweet things just as much as savoury snacks. Groups of ants can often be seen tending bugs such as aphids or treehoppers, because they love the sugary honeydew that the bugs produce. The ants stroke the bugs with their antennae to make them give off more. Then they slurp up the drops of liquid that leak out of the bugs' rear ends. Ants have such a sweet tooth that they will happily defend a group of bugs against other insects. They may even go so far as to build little shelters for the bugs in order to keep off the rain!

all the bits and pieces into its mouth. The tiger beetle lurks in a burrow until an unsuspecting creature, say a grasshopper or slug, comes near. Then it charges and pounces. The last thing the struggling victim sees is a huge pair of jaws being wielded like a set of garden shears!

K iller ants

Most ants are meat-eaters. Each day, ants catch billions of other insects. Prey is killed by being stung, bitten, or just stretched

70

Living larders

Honeypot ants dwell in dry parts of North America. When food is plentiful, the ants feed some workers with vast amounts of nectar and honeydew, making them swell to the size of beads. Their abdomens get so bloated that they never leave the nest but stay underground, hanging from the walls and ceilings like tiny pots of honey. If drought sets in and food becomes scarce, the "honeypots" vomit up drops of honeydew to feed the other ants.

Zero calories

It sounds incredible, but there are some insects that eat nothing at all after becoming adults – they survive on zero calories! An adult mayfly doesn't eat a single meal (as a youngster it lives underwater and feeds on plants). Its adult life only lasts for a day or so, and during this time it is far too busy trying to find a mate to bother with food. The mayfly's gut is full of air, making it very light – which is handy, since it spends most of its short life on the wing.

ABOUT 5 PER CENT OF ALL LEAVES ON EARTH GET EATEN BY INSECTS

ADULT MAYFLIES REACH OLD AGE BY THEIR FIRST EVENING. TO MAKE THE MOST OF SUCH A SHORT TIME ON EARTH, THEY NEVER STOP TO EAT.

INSECT WARS

N o matter how tough an insect you are, there's always something out there that can get you. Being the favourite food of so many other types of animal is bad enough. But to make things worse, insects also wage war on each other, either to satisfy their hunger or to settle disputes over territory, food, or mates. Whatever the reason, the battles can be very brutal…and often deadly.

W asps on the prowl

Hunting wasps are relatives of the hornets and common wasps that buzz around our picnics. Their stingers pack the same wallop, but they only use their weapons to slaughter other insects. When a female wasp catches her prey, the first thing she does is to inject her poison into it. This paralyzes but doesn't kill the victim. Then she carries the stiff but still-alive prey into a burrow. She lays an egg on top of the body and flies away. The whole operation is her way of doing a little advance food shopping for her baby. Later, when her larva hatches out, it will have plenty of fresh meat to eat, thanks to mum.

Hunting wasps are choosy. Some only attack spiders, while others hunt flies

A WEEVIL-HUNTING WASP PREYS ONLY ON WEEVILS. IT PARALYZES ITS VICTIMS BY STINGING THEM ON THE UNDERSIDE OF THE ABDOMEN.

LOG ON...
Watch ants live at
www.antcam.com/

WHITE SILK COCOONS SPUN BY PARASITIC WASP LARVAE HANG FROM THE BACK OF THIS CATERPILLAR'S BODY.

host's body. As well as eating their poor host from the inside out, they also use its body as a convenient place to pupate. We don't know how the host feels about all this, but one thing's certain – the hungry larvae eventually kill it.

or caterpillars. All the food that they find is saved for the kids – adults are strictly vegetarian.

Parasite perils

The best way to attack your enemy is from the inside. The larvae of many wasps are parasites, which means that they live and grow on or inside another insect's body. When it is time to lay her eggs, a female parasitic wasp deposits them on, or in, the living bodies of another insect. After the eggs hatch, the wasp larvae munch away at the delicious innards of their

Eggs within eggs

Like hunting wasps, different parasitic wasps attack different kinds of insects. Lots go for big, soft targets like the caterpillars of moths and butterflies. Others hunt the larvae of beetles and flies. Many tiny wasps, called chalcids, can't resist attacking the eggs of other insects. They lay their eggs inside eggs that were laid earlier. Their young always

A FEMALE ICHNEUMON WASP DRILLS INTO WOOD WITH HER LONG EGG-LAYING TUBE. THEN SHE LAYS AN EGG ON A BEETLE GRUB INSIDE THE WOOD.

hatch first, so they have plenty of time to eat up the egg in which they find themselves.

All-out war

Sometimes insect battles are on a grand scale, with hundreds or thousands of individuals involved. Like everything else ants do, when they go to war they set out in large numbers – and termite nests are favourite targets of many ant species. The ant raiders pour into every hole and crack in a termite nest, seizing workers and young and carrying them off to be eaten.

Although termites don't have stings, they do have their own ways of fighting back. Soldier termites are much bigger than workers and have enlarged heads. Some can dismember an ant with a single flick of their huge jaws. Others have short, flat heads that they use to plug holes in the nest and stop the raiders from getting in. Snouted termites can spray irritating chemicals from their extended snouts. There are even soldier

ANTS AND TERMITES HAVE BEEN DEADLY ENEMIES FOR MILLIONS OF YEARS. HERE, AN ANT ATTACKS A SOLDIER TERMITE.

termites that turn themselves into suicide bombers. They squeeze their abdominal muscles to fire a volley of sticky goo out of their mouths at attackers. Occasionally, the muscles may squeeze so hard that the termite's body explodes!

Ambush specialists

All this rushing around fighting is far too much effort for some insects. Many assassin bugs are ambush specialists who prefer to sit patiently on leaves, bark, or flowers, waiting for an insect to come within pouncing range. With lightning-fast reflexes, a hiding assassin bug grabs its surprised victim and plunges its long beak deep into the body to kill the prey.

Trap-setting killers

Some sit-and-wait killers set clever traps to ensure that they get their victims. To attract flies that feed on animal droppings, one type of rove beetle both looks and smells like dung. A hungry fly arriving for dinner soon finds itself being eaten as the main course!

An ant-lion is the larva of an insect like a damselfly. To catch prey, it digs a funnel-shaped pit in sandy soil. Lurking at the bottom, it hurls sand grains at passing ants and other insects, causing them to fall into the pit and straight into its spiky jaws.

Family feuds

Being attacked by complete strangers is normal in the insect world. But some insects also get into serious fights with members of their own species.

A male stag beetle patrols and defends his home patch, which is usually a log or a tree branch. This is where he courts a female and where she lays her eggs. If a rival male wanders up, hoping to steal the beetle's mate, a fight breaks out. The two males waltz about trying to grab each other around the middle with their huge jaws. The first to get a good grip lifts his opponent off the ground and flips him onto his back.

If he can, he shoves the beetle off the branch and lets him drop to the ground. The loser rarely gets killed (he has hard wing cases to protect his body) but the victor always gets the girl!

Aerial combat

A male dragonfly ferociously guards his property, which may be a stretch of riverbank or a clump of reeds. When another

STAG BEETLE FIGHTS ARE TRIALS OF STRENGTH. BUT IF THE DEFEATED BEETLE ENDS UP ON HIS BACK, HE MAY BE DEVOURED BY ANTS BEFORE HE CAN RIGHT HIMSELF.

THIS TIGER MOTH CATERPILLAR HAS A SOFT, FURRY APPEARANCE – BUT IT'S JUST A TRICK. IF YOU TOUCH IT, THE YELLOW HAIRS BREAK OFF AND STICK INTO YOUR SKIN.

male invades his territory, he circles the intruder, flashing his bright colours. If this doesn't deter his rival, a clash occurs. Sometimes, one of the males gets knocked into the water and drowns.

Noise annoys

Cracker butterflies are far more stylish. If a male cracker gets annoyed with another male in his patch, he snaps his wings violently to make a cracking sound. He dances around the intruder, snapping furiously to drive it away. The dispute is settled without any fighting or injury – just damaged pride!

Fighting back

Insects use lots of tricks to get back at the bullies and enemies that plague their lives.

New Zealand cricket, does just that. If the attacker doesn't take the hint and back off, it risks a nasty wound from the weta's spine-studded hind legs.

The next best thing is to make yourself untouchable. Some caterpillars are clad in brittle hairs that

A WETA RAISES ITS HIND LEGS IN A THREATENING POSE.

The simplest form of defence is to adopt a threatening posture. The weta, a large

77

THE BOMBARDIER BEETLE CAN SWIVEL THE END OF ITS ABDOMEN TO POINT ITS SPRAY IN ANY DIRECTION. IT CAN SWITCH THE SPRAY ON AND OFF 500 TIMES A SECOND.

The spray is made up of two harmless chemicals that the beetle stores separately in its body. When it feels frightened, it squeezes the two chemicals into a special chamber. As the chemicals combine, there is a tiny explosion that shoots a jet of hot liquid and gas from

break off easily and lodge in an enemy's skin or mouth. If swallowed, the caterpillar soon finds itself spat out again – few predators enjoy painful dinners!

C hemical defences

The most cunning tricks use chemistry. A number of insects can fire toxic chemicals at their enemies. The best chemical gun of all belongs to the bombardier beetle, which blasts attackers such as birds, toads, spiders, and ants with a boiling spray.

the tip of the beetle's abdomen with a "pop". The spray irritates and burns any animals it hits.

B listering blood

Some beetles, grasshoppers, and other insects can ooze toxic fluids from their leg joints, mouth, or rear end when grabbed by a predator. This defence tactic is called "reflex bleeding". The fluids can blister an enemy's skin and cause severe internal burns if the predator dares to eat the beetle.

WEIRD WORLD

TOXIC OIL BEETLES USE "REFLEX BLEEDING" TO DEFEND THEMSELVES. WHEN HANDLED, THEY OOZE CANTHARIDIN – A POISON SO POWERFUL THAT A DOSE OF JUST 0.03 G (0.001 OZ) IS FATAL TO HUMANS.

THIS FUNGUS BEETLE DEFENDS ITSELF BY "BLEEDING" HARMFUL CHEMICALS FROM ITS LEG JOINTS.

Hiss or squeak

Insects can't cry for help, but they can still make sounds to startle attackers. The Madagascan hissing cockroach, for example, produces a loud hiss by forcing air out of the breathing holes, called spiracles, along its abdomen. There is also a beetle, called the screech beetle, that squeaks when it is picked up.

meat-eaters steer clear of dead insects – they prefer prey to be alive and kicking. Click beetles are good at playing dead. If it's threatened, a click beetle pulls in its legs and topples off its tree to the ground. It lies there on its back, perfectly still, until the attacker goes away. If the enemy isn't fooled, the beetle hurls itself up to 30 cm (12 in) into

A BOMBARDIER'S SPRAY IS UP TO 100°C (212°F)

the air with a loud "click". The beetle makes its escape, while the bemused predator wonders what on Earth's going on!

Drop dead

If all else fails, playing dead is always worth a try. This can work because many

CLICK BEETLES CATAPULT THEMSELVES INTO THE AIR USING A SPRING-LIKE DEVICE ON THEIR BODIES.

INSECTS ON TRIAL

A re insects a good or a bad thing? If you've just been stung by a wasp or scared out of your wits by a big, hairy spider, you'll probably want to squash every insect on Earth! But before you pass judgement on these poor little critters, let's look at the evidence for and against creepy crawlies as we put insects on trial.

Accidental killer

People have lots of reasons for not liking insects – and getting bitten by them is high on the list. Most of us know how miserably painful or irritating it can be if we're bitten by midges, horseflies, black flies, bedbugs, fleas, and a host of other bloodthirsty creatures. Apart from a bite mark, some insects leave a nasty gift behind when they leave – disease.

Believe it or not, mosquitoes are the biggest killers of humans on the planet (apart from other humans, that is). Every year, mosquitoes inject malaria germs into 200 million people, while more than 3 million die of the disease. Mosquitoes don't do it deliberately. It's just that the

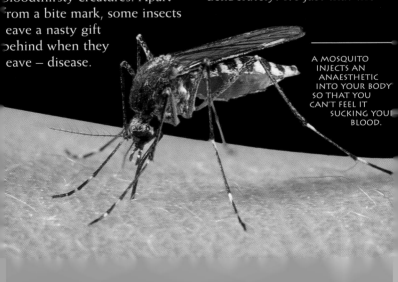

A MOSQUITO INJECTS AN ANAESTHETIC INTO YOUR BODY SO THAT YOU CAN'T FEEL IT SUCKING YOUR BLOOD.

germs accidentally get passed on from person to person when they feed on human blood. The germs are carried in saliva that the mosquito injects into the wound made by its needle-like mouthparts. It is said that every 10 seconds someone somewhere in the world dies of malaria from a mosquito bite.

Disease spreaders

Unfortunately for us, mosquitoes are just the tip of the iceberg. There are plenty of other insects that spread illness and disease among humans. Clothes lice spread typhus, tsetse flies infect people with sleeping sickness, black-rat fleas spread plague, to name just a few of the villains. Don't panic, because doctors have a whole arsenal of drugs with which they can fight these diseases. But there's a long way to go before the battle's won.

Pests indoors

Not content with attacking our bodies, insects also wreak havoc in our homes and demolish our possessions. Termites, deathwatch beetles, and woodworm beetles quite

INSECTS STINGS HURT BECAUSE THEY PUMP POWERFUL CHEMICALS INTO US. FOR EXAMPLE, A BEE STING INJECTS AN ACID, AND A WASP STING (ABOVE) AN ALKALI.

happily destroy the timbers of our homes, clothes moths eat our favourite garments, booklice munch away at our papers and books, and there's plenty of others who've got their eyes on the contents of our kitchen cupboards. And those pesky pests are also out there in gardens and farms gobbling up our crops...

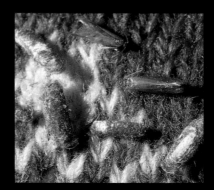

TWO CLOTHES MOTHS SIT UNSEEN ON A SWEATER. THE OVAL COCOONS SPUN BY THE LARVAE ARE CAMOUFLAGED WITH WOOL.

THE ADULTS AND LARVAE OF THE LEAF-EATING COLORADO BEETLE CAN REDUCE PLANTS TO A BLACKENED MESS.

Pests outdoors

If you were a farmer and woke one morning to find that all the buds and leaves of your potato plants were gone, then what you'd probably say as you sobbed at the sight is, "*#$!@£!* Colorado beetles!" These fat little beetles are the world's worst potato pests. Originally from western North America, they are now found wherever potatoes are an important crop. Both adults and larvae feast on the leaves of the plants, and they are very hard to control with chemical sprays.

Insects damage crops all the time. But now and then they break out as plagues that catch farmers by surprise. In 1991, in the USA, an outbreak of silverleaf whitefly in the south swept through fields of melons, tomatoes, cotton, and other crops. By the time the pest was brought under control, it had caused half a billion dollars' worth of damage to farmers.

They're not all bad

You'll be glad to hear that only 1 in 100 insect species does us any harm, and many of the rest are positively helpful to us. The most important job they do is to pollinate plants. It happens when they fly or crawl into a flower to feed. While doing it, they get dusted with pollen. When they climb into the next flower, the pollen rubs off so that new seeds and fruits can form. If insects didn't pollinate plants, we would soon starve. We'd run out of berries, plums, cauliflowers, cucumbers, and pears to start with. And you would certainly never again have apples in your lunchbox!

Pest controllers

The best way to beat back the billions of bugs that go for crops is to use other insects to prey on them. It's a lot cheaper than chemical sprays and better for the environment too. Hunters, like ladybirds and

LADYBIRDS PREY ON SOFT-BODIED INSECT PESTS. FARMERS AND GARDENERS USE THEM AS NATURAL PEST CONTROLLERS.

wasps, kill millions of aphids and caterpillars every day that would otherwise be eating what we grow.

Rubbish collectors

The other really brilliant thing that insects do is to dispose of most of the rubbish from our planet. Imagine if dung and dead plants and animals were left to lie around – we'd very soon be buried under a foul mountain of rot and poo! Luckily, plenty of insects get their kicks from devouring this unpleasant stuff.

Really useful

Insects also supply us with many useful products. Anyone who has ever slurped honey, worn a silk shirt, used food colouring, or varnished wood has insects to thank.

WEIRD WORLD

EACH YEAR, ABOUT 20 PER CENT OF ALL THE GRAIN, FRUIT, AND VEGETABLE CROPS THAT WE GROW ENDS UP IN THE BELLIES OF INSECTS. NO WONDER FARMERS SPEND SO MUCH ON PESTICIDES!

Bees make honey. Silkmoth cocoons give us raw silk. Scale insects give us a red food dye called cochineal. And some wood varnishes contain shellac, a substance that comes from another type of scale insect that lives in Southeast Asia and India. Gooey stuff, called lac, oozes out of these insects. It is gathered, washed, processed, and then used in wood varnish, or to bind together sweets and pills, or as an ingredient in printing inks.

Really tasty

Be thankful for insects – they keep lots of other animals alive because they are a never-ending source of food. Bats catch flying insects. Anteaters break open ant nests to feast on their contents. Badgers and foxes dig up juicy grubs. Lizards and frogs snap at flies. Fish gulp down any insect that lands on water. Even baby alligators munch on them.

Delicious dishes

You may find it disgusting, but many people find insects tasty, too! After all, they're rich in energy, vitamins, and minerals. In Colombia people fry up big-bottomed ants for lunch, while in Taiwan silkmoth pupae are roasted and enjoyed as a treat. Aboriginal Australians have been barbecuing beetle and moth grubs for thousands of years. It's all good healthy stuff and not so different, really, to grilling insect-like shrimps and prawns fished from the sea.

So, you see, insect and human lives are so closely interwoven that – love 'em or hate 'em – we just can't live without them.

HERE'S A NOURISHING DISH OF CATERPILLARS. NOURISHING? YES, CATERPILLARS ARE ARE UP TO 70 PER CENT PROTEIN.

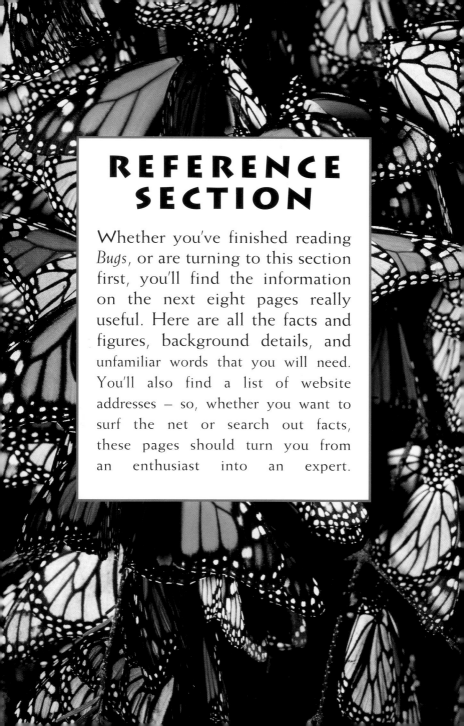

REFERENCE SECTION

Whether you've finished reading *Bugs*, or are turning to this section first, you'll find the information on the next eight pages really useful. Here are all the facts and figures, background details, and unfamiliar words that you will need. You'll also find a list of website addresses – so, whether you want to surf the net or search out facts, these pages should turn you from an enthusiast into an expert.

INSECT CLASSIFICATION

In order to discuss all the different species of plant and animal, scientists classify them into a series of categories according to the features that they share. The largest category is the kingdom. Insects are part of the animal kingdom, which also includes every other animal species. The kingdom is divided into smaller categories, which are further divided until individual species are reached. The smaller the category, the more features the animals in it have in common. The chart below shows the classification of the common red ant.

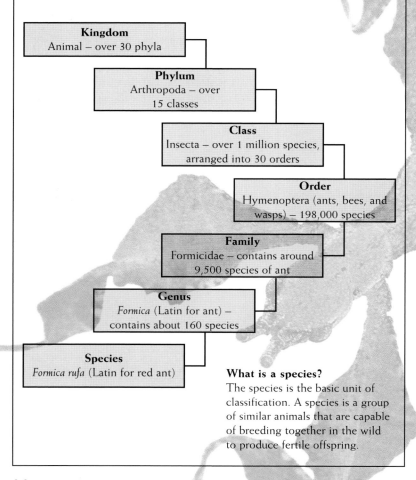

Kingdom
Animal – over 30 phyla

Phylum
Arthropoda – over 15 classes

Class
Insecta – over 1 million species, arranged into 30 orders

Order
Hymenoptera (ants, bees, and wasps) – 198,000 species

Family
Formicidae – contains around 9,500 species of ant

Genus
Formica (Latin for ant) – contains about 160 species

Species
Formica rufa (Latin for red ant)

What is a species?
The species is the basic unit of classification. A species is a group of similar animals that are capable of breeding together in the wild to produce fertile offspring.

KEY INSECT ORDERS

This chart gives details of 24 of the most important orders of insects.

NAME	MEANING	EXAMPLES	SPECIES	FEATURES
Collembola	Sticky peg	Springtails	6,500	Simple, wingless insects with a forked springing organ for jumping.
Thysanura	Bristle tails	Silverfish	370	Long, wingless insects found in dark, damp places. Run fast when disturbed.
Ephemeroptera	Live for a day	Mayflies	2,500	Larvae live in fresh water. Adults don't eat, and only live for a day or two.
Odonata	Toothed flies	Dragonflies, damselflies	5,500	Large, strong fliers with huge eyes. Larvae are fresh-water predators.
Plecoptera	Wickerwork wings	Stone-flies	2,000	Larvae live in fresh water, adults live along riverbanks. Adults eat plants or not at all.
Blattodea	Avoiding light	Cockroaches	3,700	Lurk in dark places. Will eat virtually anything. Often scavenge.
Isoptera	Equal wings	Termites	2,750	Live in huge colonies with one queen who lays all the eggs. Mostly wood-eaters.

Name	Meaning	Examples	Species	Features
Mantodea	Like a prophet	Mantids	2,000	Hunting insects with big eyes and powerful, grasping front legs.
Dermaptera	Leathery wings	Earwigs	1,900	Have pincers at end of abdomen. Fan-shaped rear wings. Will eat anything.
Orthoptera	Straight wings	Crickets, grasshoppers, locusts	20,500	Long back legs for jumping. Feed on grass. Some also chirp loudly.
Phasmatodea	Like a ghost	Stick insects, leaf insects	2,500	Flat or skinny bodies, well camouflaged to hide on foliage. Eat leaves.
Pscoptera	Milled wings	Book lice, bark lice	3,200	Small, soft-bodied insects that chew tree bark, books, and wrapping.
Phthiraptera	Louse wings	Parasitic lice	6,000	Wingless insects that live on birds and animals. Feed on blood, skin, and feathers.
Hemiptera	Half wings	True bugs	82,000	Piercing, sucking mouthparts. Feed on plants, insects, or mammals.
Thysanoptera	Fringed wings	Thrips	5,000	Tiny insects that suck plant sap. Can lay eggs without mating.

Megaloptera	Big wings	Alderflies, dobsonflies	300	Larvae are aquatic predators. Adults have long feelers and feed on plants or not at all.
Neuroptera	Net-veined	Lacewings, ant-lions	5,000	Larvae are fierce hunters. Adults are either plant- or meat-eaters.
Coleoptera	Hard wings	Beetles	370,000	Front wings form thick, horny covers for back wings.
Mecoptera	Long wings	Scorpion flies	550	Small hunting insects with biting mouthparts.
Siphonaptera	Tube with no wings	Fleas	2,400	Wingless, but have long hind legs for jumping. Suck the blood of animals.
Diptera	Two wings	Flies	120,000	Adults feed on fresh or rotting plants and animals. Larvae are legless.
Trichoptera	Hairy wings	Caddis flies	10,000	Larvae live in fresh water. Adults feed either on flowers or not at all
Lepidoptera	Scaly wings	Butterflies, moths	165,000	Adults have a long proboscis for drinking nectar. Larvae eat plants.
Hymenoptera	Membrane wings	Ants, bees, wasps	198,000	Mainly meat-eaters, but some prefer plants. Most are solitary, but others live in colonies.

INSECT RECORDS

Heaviest
Goliath beetle – up to 100 g (3.5 oz).

Longest
Indonesian giant stick insect – body 32.8 cm (12.9 in) long. Total length, including legs, of 50 cm (20 in).

Smallest
Mymarid wasps – 0.17 mm (0.0067 in).

Largest wingspan
Australian Hercules moth – 28 cm (11 in) across.

Longest antennae
New Guinea longhorn beetle – 20 cm (7.5 in).

Fastest flier
Some tropical wasps and bees – up to 72 kmh (45 mph).

Fastest wingbeat
The midge *Forcipomyia* – 62,760 beats per minute.

Slowest wingbeat
Swallowtail butterfly – 300 beats per minute.

Fastest runner
Cockroaches of the *Dictyoptera* family – 5.4 kmh (3.36 mph).

Longest jumpers
Desert locust – 50 cm (19.5 in).

Farthest migration
Painted lady butterfly – 6,436 km (4,000 miles), North Africa to Iceland.

Longest lived
Jewel beetles of the *Buprestidae* family – one was known to have lived for at least 47 years.

Shortest lived
Housefly – can complete its entire life cycle in 17 days.

Largest egg
Malaysia's *Heteropteryx dilitata* stick insect – 1.3 cm (0.5 in) long.

Longest time in the egg stage
Titanus giganteus beetle – 9.5 months.

Largest nest
Australian termite – up to 7 m (23 ft) high and 31 m (100 ft) in diameter.

Tallest nest
African termite – up to 12.8 m (42 ft).

Deepest nest
Desert termite – 40 m (131 ft) deep.

Loudest
Some cicadas and mole crickets are audible up to 1 km (0.62 mile) away.

Most sensitive sense of smell
Male emperor moth – can detect the scent of a female from more than 11 km (6.75 miles) away.

Most abundant
Springtails – up to 60,000 per sq m (5,575 per sq ft).

Insect with the deadliest poison
South African velvet ant (a type of mutillid wasp).

Most murderous
About 40,000 people are killed every year by wasp and bee stings.

Most disease-ridden
The housefly transmits more than 30 diseases and parasites.

Most deadly disease-carriers
Excluding wars and accidents, malaria carried by mosquitoes may have been responsible for 50 per cent of human deaths since the Stone Age.

Most destructive
A locust swarm can chomp through 20,000 tonnes of crops a day.

Most fertile
In theory, with unlimited food and no predators, a cabbage aphid could produce a mass of nymphs weighing 822 million tonnes in a single year.

BUG GLOSSARY

Abdomen
The rear part of an insect's body, which holds the heart, digestive system, and sexual organs.

Antennae
The two "feelers" on an insect's head that it uses to touch, taste, and smell things. They also detect vibrations.

Arthropod
An animal, such as an insect or a spider, with a jointed body-case called an exoskeleton. Arthropods do not have a backbone.

Camouflage
The way animals use shape and colour to blend in with their surroundings so that they can hide from view.

Caterpillar
The larval stage of a butterfly or moth after it hatches from an egg.

Chrysalis
A hard protective case surrounding the pupa of an insect, especially a moth or a butterfly.

Cocoon
A silk case spun around a chrysalis.

Colony
A group of ants, wasps, termites, or bees that share the same nest and are all offspring of the same mother – the queen. All the insects in the colony live and work together.

Comb
A series of cells in a bee or wasp nest arranged in rows. Food is stored in the comb and larvae are raised in its cells.

Complete metamorphosis
When an insect has distinct stages of development, from larva to pupa and finally to adult. The larva usually looks very different from the adult, and often has a different diet.

Compound eye
An insect eye made up of hundreds or even thousands of separate mini-eyes, each containing its own lens and nerve cells.

Courtship
Behaviour that leads to the selection of a mate and to mating. In insects, courtship may include making sounds, producing scents, making light, performing dance-like movements, or offering gifts.

Entomologists
Scientists who study insects.

Exoskeleton
The hard, waterproof outer shell of an insect that holds the muscles and body organs in place and gives the insect its shape. It prevents the insect's body from drying out.

Eyespots
Eye-like markings on an insect's body or wings that are used to frighten or startle predators.

Fungus garden
Fungus cultivated in a nest as food by some ants and termites.

Grub
The larval stage in the life of a young beetle, wasp, or bee.

Head
The first of an insect's three body parts. It holds the mouthparts, eyes, antennae, and, of course, the brain.

Habitat
The natural home of a living thing.

Honeydew
The sticky, sweet juice that oozes out of the rear of sap-feeding bugs such as aphids and treehoppers.

Honey guides
Patterns of lines on a flower that guide insects to the flower's nectar.
Incomplete metamorphosis
When an insect develops from a larva to an adult without becoming a pupa. The larva (nymph) looks like a small version of an adult. The larva sheds its skin many times until it reaches adult size.
Larva (plural – larvae)
The first stage of an insect's life after it has hatched from an egg.
Mammal
A warm-blooded animal with a backbone. Mammals drink their mother's milk when they are young.
Mandibles
The main pair of jaws of insects that chew their food. The mandibles have serrated edges. They move from side to side, rather than up and down.
Maxillae
The secondary jaws of chewing insects. Maxillae are mainly used to guide food into the insect's mouth.
Mimic
An insect that copies the looks and often also the behaviour of another species in order to gain protection from predators.
Nectar
A sweet liquid produced by flowers. Many insects feed on nectar.
Nymph
Another word for the larval stage of insects that develop by incomplete metamorphosis.
Parasite
An animal that feeds, lives, and grows on or in the body of another animal, called the host.
Pollen
Dust-like plant particles that contain the male sex cells of a flower. Pollen must be carried between flowers in order for fruit, nuts, or seeds to form.
Pollination
The transfer of pollen from the male part of one flower to the female part (ovary) of another flower. Plants are pollinated by insects, bats, birds, and even by the wind.
Predator
An animal that kills other animals, known as prey, for food.
Proboscis
The tube-like mouthparts of some insects that have liquid diets.
Prolegs
Muscular projections from the body of a caterpillar that help it to grip surfaces such as leaves and twigs.
Pupa (plural – pupae)
This is the resting stage of an insect that undergoes complete metamorphosis, during which it develops from a larva into an adult by a complete body change.
Queen
The founder and sole egg-laying female of a colony of ants, bees, wasps, or termites.
Saliva
A liquid secreted in the mouth that begins the process of digesting food.
Sap
A liquid that transports nutrients in plants. Many insects feed on sap.
Sense hairs
Tiny hairs on an insect's body that can detect smells, tastes, sounds, and vibrations. Each sense hair is connected to a nerve.
Simple eyes
The primitive eyes of insect larvae and some adults. They can only detect differences in light and shade.

Social insects
Those insects that live together in colonies. Ants, wasps, bees, and termites are all social insects.

Soldiers
Insects in a colony whose sole task is to defend the nest against intruders. Soldier insects cannot breed.

Species
A group of animals with similar features that can breed with one another to produce fertile young.

Spiracles
Tiny holes along an insect's body through which it breathes.

Sting
The sharp body part of some bees, wasps, or ants that is used to inject poison into prey or attackers.

Territory
An area where an insect lives and which it will defend against intruders.

Thorax
The middle part of an insect's body, to which the legs and wings attach. The thorax holds muscles for moving the legs and wings.

Ultraviolet light
Part of normal daylight that is beyond the range of human vision, but which insects can see.

Wing cases
The protective coverings of a beetle's rear wings. Wing cases are formed from the front wings, which are no longer needed for flight.

Worker
A member of an insect colony whose duties include caring for the larvae, foraging for food, and maintaining the nest. Like soldiers, workers are sterile and cannot breed.

BUG WEBSITES

www.yahooligans.com/Science_and_Nature/Living_Things/Animals/Invertebrates/Arthropods/Insects/
This excellent site lists dozens of other insect websites that are updated and checked by the editors of Yahooligans – that's the kids' section of Yahoo.

http://yucky.kids.discovery.com/
Check out the gory cockroach stuff at this Discovery Channel site. There's plenty of other yucky stuff too.

www.wnet.org/nature/alienempire/
From PBS TV, this insect site has video clips and interactive presentations.

www.pbs.org/wgbh/nova/bees/
A website about a movie made inside a beehive. Find out how the movie was made, and get a bee's-eye view of how a hive works.

www.mesc.usgs.gov/butterfly/butterfly.html
A children's butterfly site run by the US Geological Survey.

http://ant.edb.miyakyo-u.ac.jp/INTRODUCTION/Gakken79E/title.html
A Japanese photo-encyclopedia of ants with lots of in-depth information.

INDEX

CREDITS

Dorling Kindersley would like to thank:
Nomazwe Madonko and Almudena Diaz for DTP assistance; Kate Humby for proofreading; and Chris Bernstein for compiling the index.

Additional photography by:
Jane Burton, Neil Fletcher, Frank Greenaway, Colin Keates, Dave King, Kim Taylor
Thanks also to model makers Roby Baum, Jonathan Hateley, Gary Staab

DINOSAURS

THE GOOD, THE BAD, AND THE UGLY

By
Dougal Dixon

Consultant
David Lambert

A Dorling Kindersley Book

LONDON, NEW YORK, MUNICH
MELBOURNE and DELHI

Project Editor Steve Setford
Project Art Editor Peter Radcliffe
Senior Editor Fran Jones
Senior Art Editor Marcus James
Category Publisher Jayne Parsons
Managing Art Editor Jacquie Gulliver
Picture Researcher Sean Hunter
Production Erica Rosen
DTP Designers Matthew Ibbotson and Louise Paddick

This edition first published in Great Britain in 2005
First published in Great Britain in 2001 by
Dorling Kindersley Limited
80 Strand, London WC2R 0RL

2 4 6 8 10 9 7 5 3 1

The CIP Catalogue record for this
book is available
from the British Library

ISBN 1-4053-1542-3

Reproduced by Colourscan, Singapore
Printed and bound by L.E.G.O., Italy

See our complete catalogue at
www.dk.com

CONTENTS

INTRODUCTION

Dinosaurs! We see their skeletons in museums, photographs of them in books, and images of them in films and on television. But what were these amazing creatures that have so caught our imagination? And how do we know so much about them?

The name dinosaur means "terrible lizard". These creatures were land-living reptiles that dominated life on Earth about 225 to 65 million years ago, during the Mesozoic Era. The Mesozoic is often referred to as "the Age of Reptiles". Scientists have divided this part of history into three periods of time – the Triassic, the Jurassic, and the Cretaceous. You'll learn more about the world during these periods as you read this book.

Nobody knew anything about dinosaurs until about 200 years ago. Ancient peoples saw dinosaur fossils in the rocks, but they did not

STEGOCERAS WAS A SMALL DINOSAUR THAT LIVED ABOUT 70 MILLION YEARS AGO, IN THE LATE CRETACEOUS. IT ATE FRUIT, LEAVES, AND INSECTS.

understand what they were. After all, if you knew nothing about dinosaurs and discovered a limb-bone that was as long as you are, what would you make of it – a giant or a dragon perhaps? The first remains to be studied properly were found in England in the early 19th century. Soon, discoveries were being made in mainland Europe and in North America as well. Since then, dinosaur remains have been found on every continent, with the first Antarctic discoveries occurring during the 1980s.

Over the past two centuries, palaeontologists (fossil experts) and other scientists have been drawing together all the evidence. Now we think we have a good idea of what dinosaurs were and how they lived. But new discoveries often turn established ideas on their heads. It's because we keep making new discoveries and finding new evidence that dinosaur science is so exciting.

For those of you who want to explore the subject in more detail, there are black Log On "bites" that appear throughout the book. These will direct you to some terrific websites where you can find out even more. Welcome to the ever-changing world of dinosaurs!

DINO SPOTTING

You stand in an ancient forest, with unfamiliar conifer trees towering over you, the ferny undergrowth tickling your legs, and strange insects buzzing around you in the heat. In front of you, in the shade of a tree, is an animal you have never seen before. It is about your size and it is standing on its hind legs. It is a dinosaur!

Plant- or meat-eater?
What kind of dinosaur is it? As you mentally flick through all your dinosaur books, some of the names come back to you. Meat-eating *Deinonychus* and *Ornitholestes*, plant-eating *Hypsilophodon* and *Stegoceras* – all are about the same size and walk on their hind legs. But is this one a gentle plant-eater or is it a fierce meat-eater? If it likes to nibble leaves, shoots, and other vegetation, it will not bother you; if it prefers a nice big juicy steak, you are in deep trouble! The dinosaur is staring at you, so you need to find out quickly. But first you will need to check out a few things.
1. How is it standing? All meat-eaters – the dinosaur group scientists call the theropods – walked on their hind legs, using their tails for balance. But that doesn't help us much, as the main group of plant-eaters – the ornithopods – also walked on their hind legs, just as the one in front of you is doing right now.
2. Look at its jaws and teeth. If it has long jaws and sharp, pointed teeth, it is a meat-eater. If it has short jaws, with a beak

A SMALL IGUANODON IN A GLOOMY FOREST WOULD MAKE ANYONE STOP AND LOOK. AT FIRST GLANCE, HOWEVER, IT WOULD BE DIFFICULT TO TELL WHETHER THIS ANIMAL WERE DANGEROUS OR NOT.

BRACHYLOPHOSAURUS HAD A BEAK (FOR SNIPPING UP PLANTS), GRINDING TEETH BEHIND, AND A STRONG JAW HINGE. IT HAD CHEEK POUCHES AT THE SIDE, SO IT COULD CHEW GREAT MOUTHFULS OF PLANTS.

at the front and cheeks at the side, it is a plant-eater. But with its head turned towards you, it may be difficult to tell.

3. Count the fingers (if you're close enough and brave enough). Most two-footed plant-eaters had five or four fingers, whereas meat-eaters usually had three or two, and these had hooked claws.

4. The body size should be a giveaway. Meat-eaters had very slim bodies, helping them to run fast, while plant-eaters had larger, wider bodies, because they needed a bigger digestive system for the food they ate.

5. Can you see its colour? This is not a reliable guide, but meat-eaters were probably brightly coloured, striped, or spotted like

LONG-NECKED, PLANT-EATING BAROSAURUS DID NOT HAVE GRINDING TEETH. IT HAD NO WAY OF CHEWING ITS FOOD, SO IT JUST RAKED LEAFY TWIGS INTO ITS MOUTH AND SWALLOWED THEM.

MEAT-EATING ALBERTOSAURUS HAD
SHARP RIPPING TEETH, ALL DIFFERENT
SIZES AND SERRATED LIKE STEAK KNIVES.
THE JAW IS HINGED FOR CHOMPING FOOD
RATHER THAN CHEWING IT.

tigers and leopards. Plant-eaters may have been dressed in duller colours or even camouflaged.

A dangerous situation

With all this knowledge you should be able to tell what kind of dinosaur faces you. But then what do you do? A plant-eater will probably just run away, or ignore you. But if it is a meat-eater you could be in great danger – it might attack you. You've probably heard that a meat-eating dinosaur's eyes work on movement, so if its would-be prey stands still, it can't detect it. Don't believe a word of this! Scientists now know that many meat-eating

dinos had quite sophisticated senses of smell. So standing still is not a sure-fire way of keeping safe – the dinosaur can still smell you. The problem is that, although we can identify it as a meat-eating dinosaur, we don't know enough about its habits to anticipate how it might attack. From here you are on your own – so good luck!

C ut it up

Of course you'd get a better idea of what kind of animal you had if it lay dead at your feet. Then you could see its jaws and teeth, and count its fingers. If you could look inside it, what you would find would be even more interesting. Cut open the belly of the dinosaur (you wouldn't

TYRANNOSAURUS, A MEAT-
EATER, CRUNCHED BONE,
RIPPED SINEWS, AND TORE
OFF CHUNKS OF MEAT –
USING ONLY ITS JAWS.

ILIUM

ISCHIUM

PUBIS

IN BIRD-HIPPED DINOSAURS, EACH HIP CONSISTED OF A FLAT ILIUM BONE AT THE TOP AND SWEPT-BACK ISCHIUM AND PUBIS BONES.

that meat-eating dinos were probably as active as birds, so they would have needed extra oxygen to help fuel their bodies. The meat-eater's digestive system is quite small, while the liver is particularly large.

dare set off exploring in the Mesozoic Era without at least a penknife). The guts spill out. Cover your nose to avoid the stench, and use a fern frond to sweep away the flies that gather on the

LARGE INTESTINE

ILIUM

ISCHIUM

gooey mess. Yes, flies have evolved by this point in the Mesozoic, and they are just as irritating and obnoxious as they are today!

Inside a meat-eater
If this is a meat-eater, the first thing that you may notice (although we cannot be sure of this) is that there are extensions to the lungs, just like in a bird. Scientists think

PUBIS

THIS IS WHAT WE MIGHT HAVE FOUND INSIDE A MEAT-EATING THEROPOD SUCH AS CARNOTAURUS.

Inside a plant-eater
On the other hand, if the dinosaur is a plant-eater, you will find a far

12

greater volume of intestine. A plant diet needs a much more complex digestive system than a meat diet does. If you can recognize the heart among all the gore and innards, you will probably find that it is a big one, indicating that this animal, too, had an active lifestyle.

The tell-tale hips

If you are still up for it, keep cutting away the flesh beneath the legs until you

LUNG

HEART

STOMACH   LIVER

find the hip-bones. This could be the proof. In most theropod meat-eaters, the hip-bones are arranged like those of lizards, with the pubis, one of the two lower hip-bones, pointing forwards and the other, the ischium, pointing backwards. An ornithopod plant-eater has hips like those of a bird, with both the pubis and the

ischium swept backwards out of the way. This leaves a big space beneath the hips for the plant-eater's large digestive system.

Out come the scavengers

But now it's time to make a rapid exit. The smells of meat and death have alerted all the scavenging animals in the area, which start to converge on the corpse. The body is torn to bits. Flesh and organs are eaten, and the bones are carried off. The remains rot away into the soil. After some days, there is nothing left but a stain on the ground. Nothing left to fossilize. No wonder we only know of about one-fifth of the dinosaurs that ever existed!

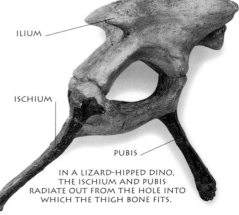

ILIUM

ISCHIUM

PUBIS

IN A LIZARD-HIPPED DINO, THE ISCHIUM AND PUBIS RADIATE OUT FROM THE HOLE INTO WHICH THE THIGH BONE FITS.

13

HOW FOSSILS FORM

S o how on Earth did any dinosaurs ever manage to become fossilized? Let's imagine a *Corythosaurus*, a plant-eater living on the wooded lowlands of western North America 78 million years ago. Our dinosaur has reached a respectable old age – perhaps 50 years, although this is just an educated guess, since scientists can't yet determine the lifespans of individual dinosaurs.

Death of a dinosaur
The *Corythosaurus* is one of several gathered by a lowland stream. The old dinosaur is frail and vulnerable to disease. As it crouches on the bank to take a drink, the great effort of lowering its head to the water

CORYTHOSAURUS HAD A DUCK-LIKE BEAK FOR STRIPPING LEAVES OFF PLANTS AND A DISTINCTIVE CREST ON ITS HEAD. IT TRAVELLED IN LARGE HERDS THROUGH PLAINS, FORESTS, AND SWAMPS.

proves too much for it. Age finally takes its toll – the blood supply to its little brain fails and life withdraws from its weary body. With a final gasp it collapses in a lifeless heap at the water's edge.

Corpse on the move

For days the rain has been falling in the mountains, and now the lowland stream is becoming swollen with mountain flood-water. The muddy torrent sweeps around the body of the *Corythosaurus*, gathers it up, and washes it downstream. Some distance away the current slows, and the heaviest of the flood debris begins to settle. The waters fall back to their normal level, and the corpse is left high and dry in the sun.

Laid to rest

The flesh of the dead dinosaur dries out quickly in the sunshine and hardens. Few scavenging animals would find this appetizing, so the body is left alone. As the corpse continues to dry out, the tendons that link the bones together shrink, pulling the neck backwards and twisting the head over the back. The limbs, too, are contorted into odd positions. Later, in the next flood, the waters swirl around the body again. By now the tendons have rotted, the

LOG ON...
In-depth fact files at
www.bbc.co.uk/dinosaurs/

A DEAD DINOSAUR FALLING INTO A RIVER
COULD SINK AND BE COVERED WITH
SEDIMENT, SUCH AS SAND, SILT, OR
MUD, BEFORE THE BODY
BEGAN TO ROT.

flesh has fallen
away, and the
skeleton has begun to break up.
The skull, a lightweight jigsaw
puzzle of interlocked bones,
collapses. A large chunk of the
tail breaks off and washes away,
as do some of the "fingers" of
the forelimbs.
Luckily, before the
skeleton is destroyed
completely, the receding
flood-water deposits a thick
layer of sediment (mostly
river sand) over the
Corythosaurus. It remains
safely buried for a long,
long, long time.

What you've just read
represents the "taphonomy" of
the dinosaur. To save you from
dashing for the dictionary,
that's the word for the study of
what happens to the body of an
animal after it dies and before
the body becomes fossilized.
The technical term for what
happens next in the fossilizing

WEIRD WORLD
THE EARTH ROTATED FASTER IN
DINOSAUR TIMES. BECAUSE OF THIS,
DAYS WERE SHORTER AND THERE
WERE 380 DAYS IN A YEAR, NOT
365 AS THERE ARE TODAY.

process is actually "diagenesis" – but to keep things simple, we'll just call it…

Turning to stone
Because the flat river plain

sea, and marine sediments, including the remains of dead sea creatures, are laid down upon it. As millions of years pass, the weight of all the sediment layers above squeezes the river sand around our

PERHAPS ONLY ONE DINOSAUR IN A MILLION WAS FOSSILIZED

where *Corythosaurus* died floods frequently, the skeleton soon becomes entombed by layer upon layer of sediment. Eventually, the land sinks beneath the

Corythosaurus skeleton. The sand particles are squashed together, so that the spaces between them become smaller and smaller. Water trickling down through the sediment

THIS FOSSIL FORMED FROM THE BODY OF AN EDMONTOSAURUS THAT DRIED AND SHRIVELLED BEFORE BEING QUICKLY BURIED.

17

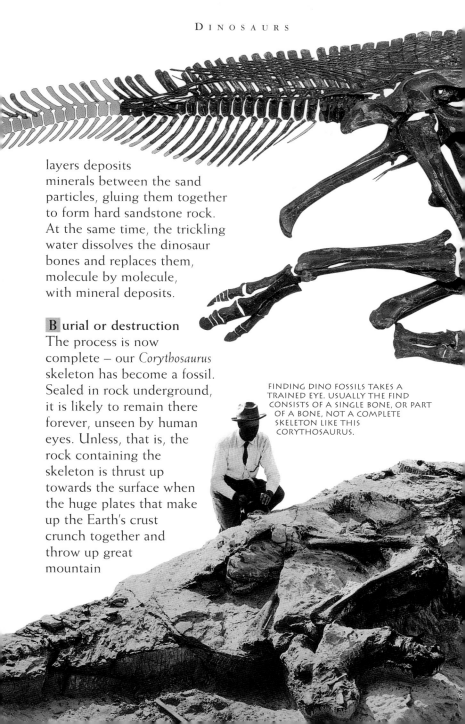

layers deposits minerals between the sand particles, gluing them together to form hard sandstone rock. At the same time, the trickling water dissolves the dinosaur bones and replaces them, molecule by molecule, with mineral deposits.

B urial or destruction

The process is now complete – our *Corythosaurus* skeleton has become a fossil. Sealed in rock underground, it is likely to remain there forever, unseen by human eyes. Unless, that is, the rock containing the skeleton is thrust up towards the surface when the huge plates that make up the Earth's crust crunch together and throw up great mountain

FINDING DINO FOSSILS TAKES A TRAINED EYE. USUALLY THE FIND CONSISTS OF A SINGLE BONE, OR PART OF A BONE, NOT A COMPLETE SKELETON LIKE THIS CORYTHOSAURUS.

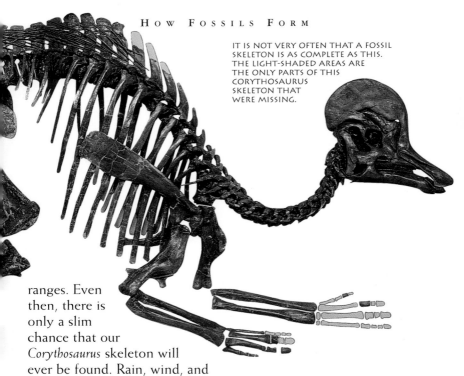

IT IS NOT VERY OFTEN THAT A FOSSIL SKELETON IS AS COMPLETE AS THIS. THE LIGHT-SHADED AREAS ARE THE ONLY PARTS OF THIS CORYTHOSAURUS SKELETON THAT WERE MISSING.

ranges. Even then, there is only a slim chance that our *Corythosaurus* skeleton will ever be found. Rain, wind, and frost soon begin to wear down the mountains, breaking up the mountain rocks and any fossils they contain, and grinding them into tiny fragments that are washed away.

Discovery

Sadly, that will be the fate of our *Corythosaurus* skeleton. The only hope is that someone passes by at just the right time – as a fossil bone is starting to emerge from the rock – and is sharp-eyed enough to realize what it is. If that person alerts a museum about the discovery, the fossil stands a good chance of being excavated and preserved. So you can see how heavily the odds are stacked against any dinosaur getting fossilized, and any fossils being discovered. We should consider ourselves lucky to have found any at all!

WEIRD WORLD
THERE ARE ABOUT 1,200 DINOSAUR SPECIMENS IN MUSEUMS. THIS SOUNDS LIKE A LOT UNTIL YOU CONSIDER THAT THERE MAY HAVE BEEN 1,500 DIFERENT DINOSAURS, EACH OF WHICH COULD HAVE LIVED FOR 2–10 MILLION YEARS…

19

THE DINOSAUR REVEALED

I magine that you have discovered a dinosaur skeleton – a *Corythosaurus* or a *Tyrannosaurus* – in sandstone rock. You will need to dig it out, but excavation takes a long time. The bones must be removed without breaking them and then transported to a place where they can be studied – a museum or a laboratory in a university.

P rotecting the bones

Although the bones have been fossilized, they are still very brittle. They must be protected while they are dug out and removed. Plaster-soaked sacking is best for this. Once you have chiselled away the over-lying rock, you must cover the exposed surface of the fossil in this material. Then you and your team – it's too big a job to tackle on your own – remove each bone or part of the skeleton completely from the rock, turn it over, and encase the rest of it in plaster.

AFTER DIGGING A TRENCH AROUND A BONE, PALAEONTOLOGISTS COAT IT IN SACKING AND RUNNY PLASTER

At every stage you photograph what you are doing to keep a record of where it all came from.

Back at the laboratory, you must take off the plaster to allow skilled technicians (called preparators) to remove any remaining rock and to treat the

fossil so that it does not decay. Now you can devote yourself to rebuilding the dinosaur. This will show you what the animal was like when it was alive.

Identification

But what type of dinosaur is it? The experts are quick to tell you that your skeleton is of a *Tyrannosaurus*. Although the ribs, the arms, most of one leg, and pieces of the skull have disappeared, your skeleton is still relatively complete. About 80 per cent of the bones are present – more than we get with most dinosaur skeletons. More than 20 *Tyrannosaurus* skeletons have been found since the first one was unearthed and named

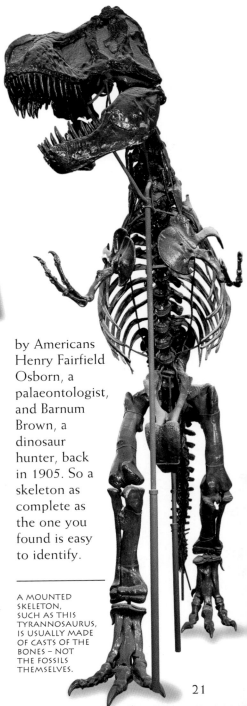

by Americans Henry Fairfield Osborn, a palaeontologist, and Barnum Brown, a dinosaur hunter, back in 1905. So a skeleton as complete as the one you found is easy to identify.

A MOUNTED SKELETON, SUCH AS THIS TYRANNOSAURUS, IS USUALLY MADE OF CASTS OF THE BONES – NOT THE FOSSILS THEMSELVES.

21

THIS TYRANNOSAURUS LEG SKELETON WILL SHOW THE MARKS WHERE THE MUSCLES WERE ONCE ATTACHED.

Dino display

If you want to put your *Tyrannosaurus* on public display in a museum, you must first decide whether to build up the skeleton with the actual fossils or with casts of them. Nowadays, it is so easy to make good casts of fossil bones from lightweight materials, such as glass fibre, that this is what is usually done. It makes the display easier to build and keeps the original fossils safe for scientific study. But what about any missing parts of the skeleton? Easy – you speak to the owners of the other 20 or so *Tyrannosaurus* skeletons and arrange to make casts of the bones missing from your own *Tyrannosaurus* skeleton.

Reconstructing and restoring

At last you have your mounted skeleton for display to the public. This is what is known as a reconstruction. Now you want to build up a picture of what the animal was like when it was alive. A painting, sculpture, or video presentation that shows what the animal was like in life is known as a restoration. The two terms are often confused.

A COMPLETE DINOSAUR SKULL, SUCH AS THIS ONE FROM TYRANNOSAURUS, IS A VERY RARE FIND. MOST SKULLS FELL APART BEFORE THEY GOT A CHANCE TO FOSSILIZE.

MODEL-MAKERS CAN USE THE LEG BONES
AND THE MUSCLE SCARS TO BUILD UP THE
LIKELY SIZE AND POSITION OF THE LEG
MUSCLES IN REAL LIFE.

The muscles

The first step in creating our
restoration is to take a close
look at the individual bones.
There are marks on them that
show where the muscles were
attached. You can compare
these with the marks on the
bones of today's animals. From
a calculation of the size and
weight of the *Tyrannosaurus*, and
of the force needed to move its
limbs, you can work out the

"FOSSIL" COMES FROM
THE LATIN FOR "DUG UP"

size of the muscles it needed.
Once you have fleshed out the
entire skeleton, you will have a
good idea of the shape of the
living animal.

Be careful with the skull. Like
most dinosaur skulls, that of
Tyrannosaurus consists of struts
of bone, and so is full of holes.
In 1920, one of the most
famous dinosaur artists of all
time, the American Charles R.
Knight, painted a *Tyrannosaurus*
with its eye in the wrong skull
hole. Few people noticed the
mistake. The painting was later

used as the inspiration
for the *Tyrannosaurus* that
appeared in the hugely
successful 1933 film
King Kong. So Knight's
error went down in
movie history.

The skin

All animals are
covered with
skin. The
dinosaurs
were, too.

23

Unfortunately, skin is too soft to be easily preserved and so it is rare to find it as a fossil. But now and again there is a lucky occurrence where a dinosaur has rolled in mud, leaving the impression of its skin behind. The impression was preserved when the mud eventually turned to rock (remember the word diagenesis?), leaving us a fossil of the dinosaur's skin texture. There is a skin impression from South America of a big meat-eating dinosaur – not *Tyrannosaurus*, but a big meat-eater of a similar size. This is the closest that we are likely to get, and so we can use this skin impression to give us an idea of the surface texture of our animal.

The colour

Finally, we must determine the colour of our dinosaur. Colour is certainly never preserved – an animal's colour hardly ever outlives the animal itself. It is one of the first things to change after the animal dies.

What we can do is look at the colour schemes worn by

THIS IMPRESSION OF CORYTHOSAURUS SKIN SHOWS THAT THE ANIMAL WAS COVERED IN SMALL, BUMPY SCALES.

modern animals. By examining an animal's lifestyle and the environment in which it lives, we can determine whether it uses its colours for camouflage, or whether it uses them to signal to other animals. We can then apply this knowledge to dinosaurs. It is possible that dinosaurs with similar lifestyles to modern animals and living in similar environments also had the same colour schemes.

A Tyrannosaurus colour scheme

A meat-eating dinosaur may have been brightly coloured, with stripes or spots, because modern hunting cats have these colour schemes. But big animals tend to be duller in colour than small animals – compare an elephant with a zebra. Taking this into consideration, we can guess that a big meat-eating dinosaur like Tyrannosaurus may have had a dull colouring consisting of stripes or spots. We may be wrong, but we've given it our best shot. It's the best we can do with the evidence available!

SCIENTISTS HAVE LITTLE EVIDENCE ABOUT DINOSAUR COLOURS. LOOK AT THESE COLOUR SCHEMES FOR THE MEAT-EATER VELOCIRAPTOR . FOR ALL WE KNOW, ANY ONE OF THEM COULD BE CORRECT.

25

DINOS GALORE!

Palaeontologists have been discovering, excavating, reconstructing, and restoring dinosaurs for about 150 years, so today we have a good idea of the range of dinosaurs that existed. We can divide the dinosaurs into two major groups, according to the arrangement of their hip-bones. One group had lizard-like hips, while the other group had hips that resembled those of a bird.

Lizard-hipped dinos

All meat-eating dinosaurs had lizard-like hips. The meat-eaters are known as theropods, a name that means "beast-footed". The 19th-century scientist who first used this name for

BARYONYX , A FISH-EATING THEROPOD, HAD A HEAD LIKE A CROCODILE. IT WAS ABOUT 10.5 M (34 FT) LONG AND 3 M (10 FT) TALL.

meat-eating dinosaurs assumed that they were predators because they had big, sharp, hooked claws on their toes. He noticed that most plant-eaters had only blunt hooves or toenails.

Theropod dinosaurs had strong hind legs

26

and long jaws bearing sharp teeth. But there was incredible variation among the dinosaurs of the theropod group.

Theropod parade

Some theropods were big and powerful, like *Tyrannosaurus*. Others were small and graceful, like the chicken-sized *Compsognathus*. In between was a vast range of dinosaurs, hunting all types of animal and using a range of strategies. There were fast little hunters, commonly called "raptors", that killed with a sickle-shaped claw on the hind foot. The raptors included the goose-sized *Bambiraptor*, the wolf-sized *Velociraptor*, the tiger-sized *Deinonychus*, and the huge *Utahraptor*.

There were fast sprinters, such as *Ornithomimus* and *Gallimimus*, that resembled ostriches. There was also a group of fish-hunting dinosaurs with crocodile-like jaws and a thumb claw for hooking fish out of the water. These included *Baryonyx* and *Suchomimus*. The earliest known dinosaurs, *Herrerasaurus* and *Eoraptor*, may have been theropods, or they may have been so primitive that they formed a different group entirely.

The sauropods

The lizard-hipped dinosaurs also included huge, long-necked

LOG ON...
www.dinofun.com for dino games, clipart, and links

WITH ITS NECK HELD UP HIGH, THE OSTRICH-LIKE GALLIMIMUS COULD SWIVEL ITS HEAD AND SEE IN ALL DIRECTIONS.

27

DIPLODOCUS WAS A SAUROPOD WITH A SMALL HEAD, WEAK JAWS, AND PENCIL-LIKE TEETH, WHICH IT USED TO RIP LEAVES OFF FERNS AND TREES.

dinos called sauropods, which means "lizard-footed".

The sauropods' enormous gut, which they needed to digest the vast quantities of plant food they ate, forced them to be four-footed. The gut had to be carried well forward of the lizard-like hips and out of the way of both forward-pointing

scientists think that the prosauropods were exclusively plant-eaters, but that they sometimes walked on their hind legs, as the theropods did, and sometimes on all fours, just like the sauropods.

BABY DIPLODOCUS WERE 2 M (6.5 FT) LONG ON HATCHING

pubis bones. This made it difficult for the sauropods to balance on their hind legs, so they went about on all fours.

Prototype sauropods
The prosauropods were an earlier group of lizard-hipped dinos that were once thought to eat both meat and

plants, thus forming a link between the theropods and the sauropods. Today,

BRACHIOSAURUS MAY HAVE BEEN AS TALL AS A FOUR-STOREY BUILDING. OTHER SAUROPODS, INCLUDING SAUROPOSEIDON , WERE BIGGER STILL.

Familiar faces

The most familiar sauropods were the long, low ones such as *Diplodocus* and *Seismosaurus*, and the tall, high-shouldered types like *Brachiosaurus* and *Sauroposeidon*. These were the most important plant-eaters in Jurassic times, but they began to die away during the Cretaceous.

One group of sauropods, the titanosaurs, survived until the very end of the dinosaur period, being particularly widespread in South America. The titanosaurs, such as *Saltasaurus*, had backs that were covered in bony armour. This was possibly to help stiffen and strengthen the animal's backbone, rather than as a defensive measure – there were few predators about that would dare to threaten a fully grown sauropod.

Bird-hipped dinos

Unlike sauropods, the bird-hipped dinosaurs could carry their plant-digesting gut beneath their hips, close to their centre of gravity. This allowed some of them, known as ornithopods, to walk on their hind legs. Ornithopod means "bird-footed".

The largest ornithopods – animals such as *Iguanodon* and the duck-billed dinosaurs *Hadrosaurus* and *Corythosaurus* – probably spent most of their lives on all fours, because of the sheer weight of their bodies. In fact, modern studies show that duck-bills' front feet were paw-like and built for taking weight. However, their youngsters were probably sprightly two-footed animals.

The smaller ornithopods, such as *Hypsilophodon*, were built for two-footed speed and were the

WEIRD WORLD
THE LARGEST OF THE SAUROPOD DINOSAURS COULD HAVE WEIGHED UP TO 100 TONNES. EXPERTS THINK THAT THE HEART ALONE MIGHT HAVE WEIGHED NEARLY 1 TONNE!

dinosaur equivalent of gazelles. The ornithopods' heyday came during the Cretaceous Period, when they took over from the sauropods as the main group of plant-eating dinosaurs.

However, many stegosaurs, including *Kentrosaurus*, only had narrow plates and spikes. These were probably used more for defence or display than for temperature control.

THERE WERE MANY MORE PLANT-EATERS THAN MEAT-EATERS

The stegosaurs
Another group of bird-hipped dinos was the stegosaurs. Also known as "plated dinosaurs", these were among the most flamboyant of the plant-eaters, with a double row of plates or spikes running along the back. These may have been used as armour or, if they were covered in skin, to control body temperature. Held towards the sun in the morning, the plates

The stegosaurs were mostly four-footed animals. Their cumbersome plates would have made it difficult for them to be otherwise. However, some of them, such as *Stegosaurus* itself, had very powerful muscles in the hip region. This would have allowed them to stand on their hind legs for short periods

may have absorbed heat and warmed the animal's blood. Held into the wind at midday, they would have given off heat and cooled the blood.

AN ORNITHOPOD, SUCH AS HYPSILOPHODON, CAN BE DISTINGUISHED FROM A MEAT-EATING THEROPOD BY ITS FATTER BODY.

so they could munch away on
low-growing branches.

The ankylosaurs

The truly armoured dinosaurs
were the ankylosaurs. These
bird-hipped dinos had bone
embedded in the thick, leathery
skin of the head, the neck, the
body, and the tail. Some of
these tough cookies were so
heavily defended that even
the eyelids were armoured,
slamming shut like the steel
shutters of a battleship when
danger approached.

Spikes, clubs, and blades

There were
two main
groups of ankylosaurs.
The first, including
Edmontonia, had spikes and
blades along the sides of the
body and tail. These spikes
were bigger in the shoulder
and neck region, and were
used to charge an enemy.

The second group is typified
by *Ankylosaurus*, which had no
spikes along its sides but
instead had a bony club on the
end of its tail. The tail bones
were fused, making the tail stiff
and strong, like the shaft of a
medieval mace. This enabled

the bony club to be swung with great force to deliver a mighty whack to the flanks and legs of an attacking theropod. Although known from early Jurassic times, it was in the Cretaceous Period that the ankylosaurs really became important, taking the place of the stegosaurs that had by then begun to die away.

The ceratopsians

The end of the Cretaceous saw the

from two-footed dinosaurs. One of the earliest examples was *Psittacosaurus*, which had a big beak and a ridge around the back of the skull, giving it a parrot-like appearance. By the late Cretaceous Period, the ceratopsians' skull ridge had extended to form an armoured shield or "frill" that protected the neck and shoulders. The later ceratopsians were divided into two groups – those, such as *Styracosaurus*, that had a large nose horn and a short frill, and those, such as

development of another group of bird-hipped dinosaurs, called ceratopsians. The ceratopsians evolved

Triceratops, that had large brow horns as well as a nose horn and a long frill. The different horn arrangements helped to distinguish one species from another as herds mixed on the North American plains.

The bone-heads

Closely related to ceratopsians were the pachycephalosaurs, which included *Stegoceras* and *Pachycephalosaurus*. What made

THE EARLIEST CERATOPSIANS, SUCH AS THE PARROT-LIKE PSITTACOSAURUS, HAD VERY LITTLE ARMOUR ON THEIR HEADS.

these two-footed plant-eaters different was the solid mass of bone on the top of the head. This "bone dome" was possibly used as a battering ram when dealing with enemies or with rivals within the herd.

Did this head-banging give them splitting headaches? We'll never know for sure, but probably not, because the bones of their skulls could be up to 23 cm (9 in) thick.

EUOPLOCEPHALUS AND OTHER LARGE ANKYLOSAURS WERE SO HEAVILY ARMOURED THAT THEY WERE LIKE WALKING TANKS.

LIFESTYLE CLUES

Now you have the mounted reconstruction of the dinosaur, and you have the restoration that shows what it looked like in life. But that is only part of the story. You need other evidence to tell you how your dinosaur lived. To find this, you must go back to the excavation site. There are plenty of clues in the sandstone rocks where you found your skeleton.

Detective work

A careful examination of the sandstone should show up bits of plant material and pollen grains. These will build up a picture of the plant life of the area. Sifting the sands may throw up tiny bones of small animals such as lizards or shrew-like mammals, or the wings of insects. These will give us an idea of what other animals existed alongside your dinosaur. Bones of freshwater fish and shells of water snails will help to prove that this was a river environment, and not a seashore one.

Footprints in the sands of time

The best evidence comes from traces left by the dinosaurs themselves. The study of fossil footprints has a

IGUANODON HAD THREE SHORT TOES ON EACH FOOT. IT WOULD HAVE LEFT CLOVER-SHAPED FOOTPRINTS ON MUD OR DAMP SAND.

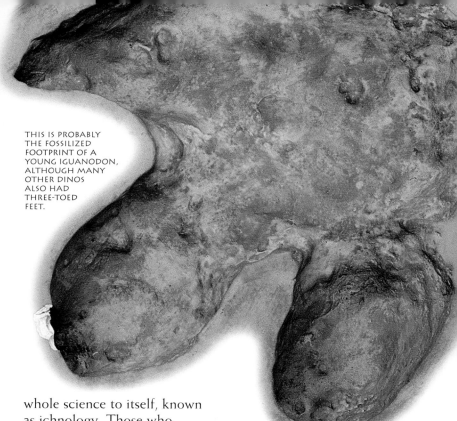

THIS IS PROBABLY THE FOSSILIZED FOOTPRINT OF A YOUNG IGUANODON, ALTHOUGH MANY OTHER DINOS ALSO HAD THREE-TOED FEET.

whole science to itself, known as ichnology. Those who study fossil footprints (ichnologists) claim that their science reveals more about the living dinosaur than any number of bones can. You can see their point. In its lifetime a single animal can leave thousands of footprints behind, but only one skeleton. From the footprints, we can tell if an animal has been walking or running. If running, we can estimate the speed. We can tell if it had been travelling along a

A PALAEONTOLOGIST EXAMINES FOSSILIZED DINOSAUR FOOTPRINTS. THE SPEED OF THE ANIMAL CAN BE CALCULATED FROM THE DISTANCE BETWEEN ITS FOOTPRINTS.

river bank, crossing a river, or gathering around a water hole. We can tell if it moved about singly, in a pair, in a family group, or as part of a herd. What we cannot tell, however, is exactly which dinosaur made which set of footprints. We can have a good guess, but there will always be an uncertainty. That is why ichnologists give fossil footprints their own scientific names. *Brontopodus* may be the footprints of a sauropod like *Apatosaurus*, but we are not sure.

Tetrapodosauropus may be the footprints of an armoured dinosaur like *Nodosaurus*, but we cannot be 100 per cent certain.

Dinosaur eggs

How do you like your eggs – fried, scrambled, or boiled? Palaeontologists prefer theirs to be fossilized! Dinosaur eggs, although rare, give us another

MAIASAURA MEANS "GOOD MOTHER LIZARD". SCIENTISTS THINK THAT FEMALE MAIASAURA BROUGHT FOOD TO THEIR NEWLY HATCHED BABIES.

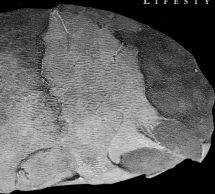

THE FIRST EGGS DISCOVERED WERE THE SIZE OF COFFEE MUGS. PALAEONTOLOGISTS WRONGLY ASSUMED THAT THEY WERE PROTOCERATOPS EGGS.

Oviraptor is innocent!
The first dinosaur eggs were found in the Gobi Desert, Mongolia, in the 1920s by an expedition from the American Museum of Natural History. Among fossilized herds of the horned dinosaur *Protoceratops*, they found nests of eggs. During the late Cretaceous, the eggs had been laid in a circle in a hole scooped in sand. One even had the skeleton of a small theropod crouched over it. The theropod was named *Oviraptor*, or "egg thief", as it seemed to have died in the act of raiding a

glimpse into dinosaur life. Once again, there is a great deal of difficulty in matching eggs to particular dinosaurs. Sometimes we are lucky and find whole nesting sites with nests, eggs, babies, and adults, all fossilized together.

Perhaps the best-known nesting site is in Montana, USA. It is the nesting site of the duck-billed *Maiasaura*. The nests, built of mud and twigs and about 2 m (6.5 ft) across, are spaced at regular distances from each other. In or by the nests are egg shells, baby dinosaurs, partly grown dinosaurs, and adults. Experts believe that this represents an annual nesting site, to which the *Maiasaura* herd migrated every year. More often, the evidence is vague or misleading.

Protoceratops nest. Seventy years later, another such nest was found in Mongolia. This nest contained the

THIS IS THE SKULL OF PROTOCERATOPS, A FOUR-LEGGED PLANT-EATER WITH A LARGE BONY NECK FRILL FOR PROTECTION AND A SHARP BEAK FOR SNIPPING UP VEGETATION.

THIS SKELETON OF AN OVIRAPTOR SITTING ON THE GOBI DESERT EGGS SHOWS THAT THESE EGGS WERE NOT FROM PROTOCERATOPS AFTER ALL.

ARM

CLAWS

EGGS

FOOT

same eggs, but this time an *Oviraptor* was sitting upon them, brooding like a modern bird. The eggs were found to have *Oviraptor* embryos inside them. So the eggs found in the 1920s were *Oviraptor* eggs all the time!

In a similar story, some large eggs found in southern France were, for a long time, attributed to the sauropod *Hypselosaurus*. But recently it has been suggested that they were actually laid by a big cassowary-like bird that lived in France at about the same time as *Hypselosaurus*. So you see, some of what we know today about dinosaurs may be overturned by what we discover in the future.

Dinosaur droppings
Coprolite. There is an impressive name. It actually means "dung stone". A coprolite is the fossil of an animal's droppings! Coprolites may sound like repulsive remains to you, but palaeontologists love them, and some devote themselves entirely to studying this prehistoric poo. The most common coprolites come from aquatic animals such as fish, but

OVIRAPTOR HAD A STRANGE FACE, WITH A SHORT BEAK THAT SEEMED TO SUGGEST IT WAS AN EGG-EATER. NOW WE ARE NOT SO SURE.

LOG ON...
See Zoom Dinosaurs at www.enchantedlearning.com

several dinosaur coprolites have been found. Food fragments in a coprolite can tell us about the diet of its "owner", and the coprolite's shape can reveal something about the layout of the animal's digestive system.

There is one coprolite that is thought to be *Tyrannosaurus* dung, but as with footprints and eggs, it is impossible to be sure. It is 20 cm (8 in) long and full of pieces of duck-billed dinosaur bones – just what we'd expect from guessing about *Tyrannosaurus'* hunting habits.

S tomach stones

Another guide to the diet of a dinosaur is the presence of stomach

stones, or gastroliths, in the skeleton. The sauropods did not have the type of teeth that could be used for chewing. Instead, they raked leaves and twigs from branches and swallowed them whole. To help them process their food,

they also swallowed stones. These gathered in an area of the stomach called the gizzard and helped grind up the food as it passed through. Today, plant-eating birds such as pigeons swallow grit for the same purpose – they cannot chew with their beaks. Gastroliths may be found with the fossilized skeletons of sauropods. They may also appear as neat piles where the animals vomited them up when they became too smooth to be of any use. New, rougher stones were then swallowed to keep the grinding process going.

COPROLITES MAY JUST LOOK LIKE STONES TO US, BUT TO PALAEONTOLOGISTS THEY'RE TREASURE TROVES OF DINO INFORMATION.

WEIRD WORLD

A DINOSAUR TRACKSITE IN TEXAS, USA, COVERS AN AREA OF 100,000 SQ KM (38,600 SQ MILES). IT IS ONLY SEEN ON THE SURFACE IN A FEW PLACES – THE REST IS BURIED IN THE ROCKS.

OTHER LIFE AT THE TIME

B y this stage, you may be thinking that dinosaurs were practically the only creatures on Earth during the Mesozoic Era. Far from it – there was a whole host of other animals around at the time. As with the dinosaurs, it's through fossils that we know of their existence.

AMMONITES WERE TENTACLED SEA CREATURES WITH SPIRAL-SHAPED SHELLS. FOSSILIZED AMMONITES ARE COMMON IN MARINE ROCKS FROM DINOSAUR TIMES.

Water beasts

We have already seen how difficult it is for a land animal such as a dinosaur to become fossilized. The best dinosaur fossils come from animals that lived near water, because their dead bodies could become buried in sediment and involved in the rock-forming processes. How much easier, then, must it be for an animal that actually lived in the water to become fossilized. If you go out and look for fossils in a well-known fossil site, you'll rarely find the fossil of a dinosaur or any other large animal. What you will find are the fossils of shellfish and other animals that lived in the sea. It's not surprising, really. Shellfish live on the sea bed, where sediments

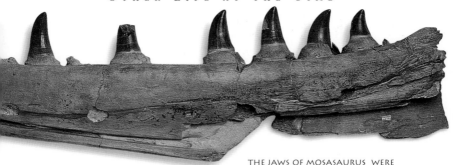

THE JAWS OF MOSASAURUS WERE LINED WITH SHARP CONICAL TEETH. THIS REPTILE SWAM IN SHALLOW COASTAL WATERS AND WAS UP TO 10 M (33 FT) LONG.

are continually accumulating, so their remains naturally get buried under sand, mud, or silt.

The first sea monster

The Mesozoic was truly the Age of Reptiles. Not only were dinosaurs masters of the land, but reptiles also dominated the seas and commanded the skies. The Mesozoic sea reptiles were known to scientists long before the dinosaurs were. In 1770, a fossilized jaw was unearthed in a chalk mine near Maastricht in the Netherlands. It fell into the hands of the invading French army and eventually ended up

in Paris, where it was studied by Baron Georges Cuvier, the leading biologist of the day.

At that time, scientists were beginning to understand that different animals had lived on the Earth at different times, and that many of the animals that lived in the past were now extinct. Cuvier realized that the fossil skull was from a type of enormous swimming lizard, which became known as *Mosasaurus*. This was one of a

WE KNOW THAT THE FISH LEPIDOTES LIVED DURING DINOSAUR TIMES, BECAUSE ITS SCALES HAVE BEEN FOUND IN THE STOMACH OF BARYONYX .

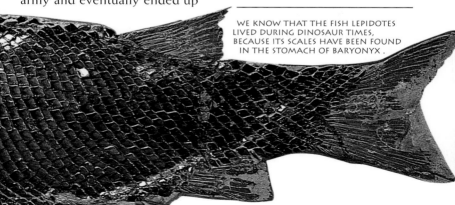

large family of reptiles, called the mosasaurs, which swam by thrashing their tails to and fro. The other big reptiles of the Mesozoic were ichthyosaurs and plesiosaurs. On the coast of Dorset, in southern

THE PLESIOSAUR CRYPTOCLIDUS HAD A SNAKE-LIKE NECK AND INTERLOCKING SPIKED TEETH THAT CLAMPED TIGHT AROUND FISH AND OTHER SEA CREATURES.

England, skeletons of these marine reptiles were being dug up and studied in the early 19th century.

Fishy lizards

The ichthyosaurs, or fish lizards, were originally regarded as a type of crocodile.

It is easy to see why, with their long jaws and sharp teeth – the signs of a meat-eating reptile. But when more and more skeletons were discovered, it became clear that they were a totally different kind of animal. Although they were reptiles, they were so well-adapted to their watery way of life that they developed body shapes

WEIRD WORLD

WHEN A BASKING SHARK DIES, ITS HUGE JAWS FALL OFF. THE TINY-HEADED CARCASS LOOKS LIKE A ROTTING PLESIOSAUR. THIS EXPLAINS REPORTS OF DEAD PLESIOSAURS BEING FOUND ON MODERN BEACHES.

ICHTHYOSAURUS SWAM WITH SIDEWAYS MOVEMENTS OF ITS TAIL. LIKE OTHER MARINE REPTILES, IT HAD TO SURFACE TO FILL ITS LUNGS WITH AIR.

just like those of fish or dolphins – a streamlined body, paddles for limbs, a fin on the tail and one on the back. The fins were not originally obvious, but fossil ichthyosaurs discovered near Holzmaden, in Germany, were so detailed that even these soft body parts were preserved. The ichthyosaurs evolved in the Triassic, when some grew as big as whales. They flourished in the Jurassic and died out before the end of the Cretaceous, when they were replaced by the mosasaurs.

Long necks and short necks

There were two types of plesiosaur. The long-necked types which, according to one 19th-century scientist, resembled snakes threaded through turtles, and the short-necked types, which had big heads and long jaws. Again, these are much more common as fossils than land-living animals such as dinosaurs. They evolved in the Triassic and continued until the end of the Cretaceous Period.

Flying reptiles

As well as reptiles powering through the oceans, there were also reptiles flapping, soaring, and swooping through the sky. The pterosaurs were a group of reptiles that, although distantly related, were not themselves dinosaurs. Their wings were thin flaps of skin supported by elongated fourth fingers. Pterosaurs probably ate fish and insects, and may have been covered in fur, like bats are today. We have a fair number of pterosaur

fossils, because many of them lived in coastal areas and fell into the sea when they died.

For the first part of the Age of Reptiles, these animals were the undisputed rulers of the skies, with flying insects their only competitors. But in the Jurassic Period, birds evolved

DIMORPHODON PROBABLY SNATCHED FISH IN ITS PUFFIN-LIKE BEAK AS IT SKIMMED LOW OVER THE SEA. THE LONG TAIL GAVE STABILITY IN THE AIR.

from dinosaur ancestors, and by Cretaceous times these feathery newcomers shared the skies with the pterosaurs.

PTERODACTYLUS HAD A WINGSPAN OF ABOUT 50 CM (20 IN). LIKE OTHER PTERODACTYLOIDS, IT HAD A SHORT TAIL AND LONG WRIST-BONES.

The first pterosaurs, the rhamphorhynchoids, had long tails and narrow wings, and included the big-beaked *Dimorphodon*. Later pterosaurs, called pterodactyloids, had short tails and broader, more controllable wings. The pterodactyloids produced the biggest flying creatures Mesozoic Era, but the most important group of vertebrates were the little furry things that scampered around the feet of

PTEROSAURS HAD LIGHTWEIGHT HOLLOW BONES FILLED WITH AIR

that ever lived – some the size of small aeroplanes – during the Cretaceous Period.

L esser lights

We have looked at the main groups of reptiles that shared the world with the dinosaurs. A vast array of other animals lived at the time, too. The lizards and snakes evolved in the

the reptilian giants…the mammals. The mammals evolved in the late Triassic Period, at about the same time as the dinosaurs. Throughout the Age of Reptiles they were small, insignificant, shrew-like animals. It was not until the dinosaurs died out that the mammals came into their own. But that is another story.

45

DINOSAUR HOMES

Y ou've seen how palaeontologists put together the pieces of the dinosaur jigsaw to give us a picture of life in Mesozoic times. We know what dinosaurs looked like, what they ate, how they walked, and what their eggs were like. But the picture is incomplete, as we are less certain about which dinosaurs lived in which habitat.

Where dinosaurs lived

Scientists reckon that dinosaurs colonized all the major habitats of the Mesozoic world. It's difficult to be more precise than that because many habitats were not suited to fossil formation. What do we know, for example, about dinosaurs that lived on mountain tops, where the landscape was constantly being eroded? Practically nothing. What do we know of dinosaurs that lived on windswept rocky outcrops, where no sediments could be laid down? Zilch! What do we know of dinosaurs

LIKE BARYONYX, SUCHOMIMUS WAS A FISH-EATER THAT LIVED BESIDE RIVERS AND LAKES.

that lived in forests well away from rivers, where the soil was continually renewing itself with the growth and decay of plants? Not much more. On rare occasions, we find a dinosaur that was fossilized under ideal circumstances, and from which we can learn a lot.

B y the river

Take *Baryonyx*, for example. Nothing like it had ever been found before its discovery in 1983 in a clay pit in Surrey, south-eastern England. It was found in river sediments by an amateur fossil collector. It was about half complete, but the bones that were present were enough to tell experts what the

WEIRD WORLD
HALF AN *AMMOSAURUS* SKELETON WAS FOUND BY WORKERS BUILDING A BRIDGE IN CONNECTICUT, USA, IN THE 1880S. THE REST WAS FOUND A CENTURY LATER WHEN A NEARBY BRIDGE WAS DEMOLISHED!

whole skeleton would have been like. *Baryonyx* had long jaws with many sharp teeth, just like a fish-eating crocodile. It also had a big claw on its thumb that resembled the hook on a fishing rod. What's more, its stomach was full of fish bones and fish scales, so it was clear what it ate. The Cretaceous sediments in which

THESE ENTWINED SKELETONS SHOW HOW A PROTOCERATOPS AND A VELOCIRAPTOR FOUGHT EACH OTHER TO THE DEATH MORE THAN 70 MILLION YEARS AGO.

with its thumb claws – just like a modern grizzly bear.

Close relative

Baryonyx was so unusual-looking that when an almost identical animal, *Suchomimus*, was found in North Africa in 1997, scientists had absolutely no doubt that it had lived in the same kind of habitat and had the same lifestyle as *Baryonyx*. But *Suchomimus* was bigger and had a low fin down the length of its back. It was still a closely related animal that waded in rivers to hunt fish.

it was found were laid down on a boggy plain populated by ornithopod dinosaurs such as *Iguanodon* and *Hypsilophodon*. So here we have an instant picture of *Baryonyx*. It was a fish-eating theropod wading in shallow rivers and hooking out fish

WEIRD WORLD
ADULT HUMANS HAVE JUST 32 TEETH, BUT A HADROSAUR HAD UP TO 2,000! LIKE OTHER DINOSAURS, A HADROSAUR COULD REPLACE WORN AND DAMAGED TEETH THROUGHOUT ITS ENTIRE LIFE.

VELOCIRAPTORS MAY HAVE HUNTED IN PACKS SO THAT THEY COULD TACKLE LARGE PREY. THEY PROBABLY ENCIRCLED VICTIMS BEFORE POUNCING, SLASHING AWAY WITH SICKLE-SHAPED CLAWS ON THEIR REAR FEET.

LOG ON...
Classic dino pictures at
www.search4dinosaurs.com

Secrets of the sands

Another snapshot of dinosaur life was developed in 1972. An expedition in the Gobi Desert in Mongolia uncovered the complete skeletons of a horned *Protoceratops* and a meat-eating *Velociraptor* wrapped around one another. Tickle your cat on its tummy. What does it do? It grabs your hand and kicks away with its hind claws. That's exactly what happened here. The *Velociraptor* had seized the head-shield of the *Protoceratops* and was slashing away at it with the killing claws of its feet. The *Protoceratops* had responded by seizing the attacker by the arm with its sharp beak.

The fierce struggle was fatal for both dinosaurs. A sandstorm then buried the pair, and they were preserved until the present day.

Desert dwellers

This gruesome scene tell us that early horned dinosaurs such as *Protoceratops* were prime targets for the predators of the time. But they certainly didn't give in without a fight! We also know, from the numbers of remains buried in sandstorm deposits, that *Protoceratops* was one of the most common animals around, dotting the

49

GIGANOTOSAURUS WAS UP TO 12.5 M
(41 FT) LONG AND 8 TONNES IN WEIGHT.
WE KNOW LITTLE OF ITS LIFESTYLE.

landscape like sheep feeding
on the sparse desert vegetation.
Other fossil finds imply that
Velociraptor may have lived and
hunted in packs.
If we

imagine a *Velociraptor*
pack prowling the
desert on the lookout
for a lone *Protoceratops*
that has wandered
away from the
herd, then
we are
probably
not far from
the truth.

Forest hunter

Usually it's more difficult to say for certain where a dinosaur lived. We can look at the partial skeleton of *Giganotosaurus*, found in South America, and deduce that it must have been one of the biggest meat-eating dinosaurs. We can conjure up a vision of it rampaging through coniferous forests during the Cretaceous Period. We can also imagine it preying on the biggest plant-eaters that ever lived – such as the sauropod *Argentinosaurus*, which lived in South America at the same time. We really do not have too much evidence for this scenario, however.

Plains runner

Then there are the skeletons of the "ostrich-mimic" dinosaurs, such as *Gallimimus*. These lightly built Cretaceous theropods are known as the ostrich mimics because of their rounded

OSTRICHES RUN FOR LONG DISTANCES OVER DRY PLAINS, TRAVELLING FROM ONE FEEDING GROUND TO ANOTHER.

bodies and their long necks and legs. (But this comparison conveniently ignores *Gallimimus*'s long tail.) Recent studies suggest that the resemblance between ostriches and ostrich-mimic dinosaurs is superficial, but the idea won't go away. We see photographs of ostriches sprinting across the open plains of Africa, and it's easy to imagine herds of *Gallimimus* doing the same. Perhaps they did. But, as is often the case, hard evidence is lacking.

GALLIMIMUS MAY HAVE RUN AT UP TO 80 KMH (50 MPH) – FASTER THAN A RACEHORSE.

TRIASSIC TREK

L et us take a walk in the late Triassic Period (about 215 million years ago), after the first dinosaurs had evolved. We know enough from the palaeontology and geology of the time to be able to imagine this. We had better start our walk by the sea. It is the only place that we would find comfortable, or even remotely habitable.

A different world

The late Triassic world is very different from the one we know. If we wanted to go from, say, Los Angeles, USA, to Sydney, Australia, in the 21st century, we would have to fly or sail across the ocean spaces

THERE WERE NO FLOWERING PLANTS OR BROAD-LEAVED TREES IN THE TRIASSIC, BUT THERE WERE PLENTY OF HORSETAILS, FERNS, CONIFERS, AND PALM-LIKE PLANTS.

in between. But in Triassic times we could walk there, if we had enough time and energy. All the landmasses are united as a single giant supercontinent, called Pangaea. Pangaea is so vast that most places in the interior are a long way from the moisture and cooling influences of the sea, so they are fiercely hot and dry. But don't worry, we won't even contemplate such an arduous journey – we'll stick to places that are less hostile.

By the seaside

The air is both moist and cool by the sea, but you know that over the dusty hills you can see inland there are vast swathes of

THE TRIASSIC GLOBE. THE TETHYS SEA, A BRANCH OF THE OCEAN PANTHALASSA WOULD LATER SPLIT PANGAEA IN TWO.

CYCADS ARE
SQUAT PLANTS
LIKE PALMS.

arid desert.
Huge waves
pound against
the beach.
They have had
a long distance
to travel across
Panthalassa – that's what we
call the vast ocean that covers
the rest of the Earth's surface.
Great for surfing!

At your feet, the tide-line
consists of shells that you have
never seen before. These are
mostly coiled ammonite shells,
whose empty chambers once
held octopus-like marine
animals. The tangle of seaweed
looks pretty much the same as
that from your own time.

and cycads. They
must have come
from a river that
empties into the
sea somewhere
close by.

Don't touch
dead things
What's that smell? In the
distance lies the body of a giant
ichthyosaur, like a beached
whale. Long-tailed pterosaurs
wheel around it and squabble
over the decaying flesh.
Lobster-like creatures scuttle
over the corpse. The stench is
strong enough to convince you
not to go anywhere near that
nasty mess. Leave them to their
feast. You have come here
because you
want

Among the seaweed are
washed-up tree branches,
mostly from conifers, ginkgoes,

to see dinosaurs, so let's go
inland and do some exploring.

WEIRD WORLD
IN OUR TIMES, BIG ANIMALS TEND
TO LIVE LONGER LIVES. SOME
SCIENTISTS SUGGEST THAT
TYRANNOSAURUS MAY HAVE LIVED
FOR 100 YEARS, AND THE
BIGGEST SAUROPODS UP TO 200.

River safari
We walk up the bank of a river.
Here, where there is moisture,
there is also plenty of life.
Conifers line the riverbanks,
their roots in an undergrowth
of ferns and mosses. Between
the tree-trunks we see the
desert spreading away to the
horizon. There's a rustle in

the undergrowth, and
a little animal scampers
away. A dinosaur?
No, it is furry and has
whiskers and little
ears, like a mouse.
It is one of the
first mammals.

small body, long
hind limbs, balancing
tail, long jaws, and sharp teeth.
It is probably *Herrerasaurus*, one
of the earliest known dinosaurs.

Our first dinosaur

Suddenly there's a lunge and a
snap! Something snatches the
mammal from the ground and
shakes it to death. We can see
the culprit clearly – it's our first
dinosaur! The dinosaurs and the
mammals have both recently
evolved,

Giant newts

Upstream we go. The
vegetation on either side is
getting thinner as the desert

encroaches. In
the backwaters and
swamps we see the murky
waters swirl. Aquatic
dinosaurs? You know better
than that! There were no
aquatic dinosaurs. These are
giant amphibians, like newts as
big as alligators. The time of
large amphibians is almost past,
but there are still plenty of
them here. They seem to be
settling into the mud as if they
are preparing to weather out
some dry times ahead.

but it's clear from
this encounter which
is the more powerful.
The dinosaur turns and
runs off between the
trees, carrying
its limp prey.
We note the
dinosaur's

HERRERASAURUS WAS A PRIMITIVE
MEAT-EATING DINOSAUR, ABOUT 3 M
(10 FT) TALL. IT HAD A SLENDER BODY,
NARROW JAWS, AND POWERFUL BACK LEGS.

A pack of mischief

There is movement beyond the ferns. We push through the fronds to see a whole pack of *Coelophysis* scampering about, dipping their snouts between the ferns to snap up insects and snails. *Coelophysis* are very long, maybe as long as a family car, but most of the length is tail and neck. In body size they are no bigger than modern turkeys. Their forage path leads them away from the river to the sandy plain with its scattered clumps of fern. The season is changing and there is not enough food to be found beside the river.

A hungry journey

For days they trek across the wilderness, instinctively knowing the direction in which food lies. Now and again they trek across a drying pond, leaving three-toed footprints that will be fossilized in desert sandstone. The ferns become scarcer, and each clump that the pack finds is ripped apart for any insects that it may hide. But small stuff like this will not satisfy their hunger.

Eventually they reach a valley, where a drying river winds its muddy way through stunted trees. A group of bigger animals lives here. From their massive bodies and long necks we recognize them as prosauropods, probably *Plateosaurus*.

Food at last!

Have you ever seen a healthy elephant attacked by a tiger? No. And you never will. There's something about really big animals that deters even the fiercest predators. These *Plateosaurus* are big, too, which is why the *Coelophysis* leave them alone. Suddenly there's a frantic bellowing nearby. An enfeebled old *Plateosaurus* is stuck in the mudflats and can't get out. This is more like it – a plant-eater in trouble! Instantly the *Coelophysis* pack sets upon the hapless beast. Tearing at its long throat and tall flanks, they soon bring down the defenceless animal. Let's not look, it will be too horrible. That prosauropod is history – or even prehistory! But the *Coelophysis* will have meat for many a day.

COELOPHYSIS WERE SLIM, AGILE PACK ANIMALS THAT WERE BUILT FOR SPEED. WHEN FOOD WAS SCARCE, THEY SOMETIMES HAD TO EAT THEIR OWN YOUNG.

JURASSIC JAUNT

We are scuba diving…in the Jurassic sea! Although it is more than 150 million years ago, under the waves we see the same white sand and the same clear blue water that we see off the Bahamas in our own time. We are swimming in one of the shallow seas that is spreading over low-lying areas as Pangaea begins to break up.

IN THE JURASSIC, THE SUPERCONTINENT OF PANGAEA BEGAN TO SPLIT INTO FRAGMENTS THAT SLOWLY DRIFTED APART.

TETHYS SEA

PANGAEA

PANTHALASSA

vanish into the distance. They must have been belemnites. Disc-shaped ammonites drift around more sedately, their big eyes looking out for prey. They are ignoring us – we're far too big for them.

A warm dip in the ocean

The main difference we notice is in the shoals of swimming animals around us. Unfamiliar fish nibble on the coral growing through the sand. Bullet-shaped things that look like squid weave past us and

PLESIOSAURS PROPELLED THEMSELVES GRACEFULLY THROUGH THE WATER, WITH SLOW BEATS OF THEIR HUGE FLIPPERS.

Jurassic jaws

What's that dark shadow passing over us? It's an ichthyosaur on the prowl. It is a smaller, more streamlined ichthyosaur than the whale-like creature we saw washed up on the Triassic beach. The ammonites draw in their tentacles and, with a

ABOUT 7 M (23 FT) LONG, A PLIOSAUR WAS A FIERCE OCEAN HUNTER OF FISH AND SMALL SEA REPTILES IN THE LATE JURASSIC.

squirt of ink, dart away. However, the ichthyosaur is not after them. With a flip of its tail it cruises away in the direction of the departing belemnite shoal.

S ea serpents

Let's rise through the water and see what we can find. Hold still! There is something else here – a pair of plesiosaurs cruising just below the surface. Don't panic! Control your breathing or you won't be able to see through the bubbles. And try not to be noticed. It's OK, the plesiosaurs are more interested in fish. With

lazy, wing-like flaps of their paddles they move slowly through the water. Their heads, on their long necks, are turning this way and that, their long teeth ready to snap at any fish that comes within range.

R eptiles of the sky

We break the surface. Luckily we are not far from the shore. The landscape seems to be low-lying and thickly vegetated. Dark shapes are wheeling in the sky, as we would expect seagulls to do. Watch out for coprolites

dropping from the sky! But these are not seagulls. Their big heads and leathery wings show them to be pterosaurs. We can spot both long-tailed and short-tailed types. Perhaps there are no birds at this time?

undergrowth and flaps clumsily towards the low-hanging branches of a conifer tree. It is *Archaeopteryx*, the first bird. It settles on a branch on all fours – it has claws on its "hands" as well as its feet – because it is

ARCHAEOPTERYX PROBABLY ONLY MADE SHORT GLIDING FLIGHTS

Beachcombers

On the beach we see a little chicken-sized dinosaur scampering along the sand, pursuing a lizard. It must be *Compsognathus*, because

not very good at perching. The flustered *Archaeopteryx* screams loudly at the reptiles in the undergrowth. So there are birds here after all!

that's the smallest Jurassic dinosaur we know of. The lizard weaves and dodges up the beach, disappearing beneath the arching fronds of the ferny undergrowth. The *Compsognathus* gives chase. Suddenly a dreadful squawking erupts from the foliage. A feathered form leaps disturbed from the

Green landscape

Ready to go into the forest? It could be dangerous. The vegetation, as in the Triassic, consists of conifer and ginkgo trees and cycads,

AGILE AND QUICK-FOOTED, COMPSOGNATHUS ATE CREATURES SUCH AS SNAILS, LIZARDS, INSECTS, AND FROGS.

ARCHAEOPTERYX WAS A PRIMITIVE BIRD WITH TEETH, A BONY TAIL, WEAK FLAPPING MUSCLES, AND CLAWS ON ITS WINGS.

with an undergrowth of horsetails and ferns. However, there seems to be so much more of it. The air is much moister than it was during the dry Triassic, and the land is much greener. The oceans that are creeping in along the deep valleys formed by the splitting of Pangaea, and the shallow seas that are spreading over the land, are producing wetter climates. In fact, it is beginning to rain.

The forest browsers

Pushing onwards through the wet forest, knee-high in sodden ferns and with dripping boughs splashing cold drops on our heads, we suddenly find ourselves in an open clearing. A herd of huge beasts stands at one end of the clearing, their long necks reaching about like vacuum-cleaner hoses to munch the undergrowth as they go. The clearing is caused by them ripping up the vegetation. They are obviously sauropods of some kind, probably *Barosaurus* or one of the other long, low types.

There are about a dozen *Barosaurus* in the herd. Now and again, they reach up to scrape needles from one of the conifer trees. Their teeth seem to be designed to feed both high and

61

LOG ON...
has a useful "Dino Directory"
www.nhm.ac.uk/

THE HOSTILE DESERTS BEGAN TO DISAPPEAR DURING THE JURASSIC, BUT THE CLIMATE WAS STILL WARMER THAN IT IS TODAY.

low. They have heard us. One, obviously the leader of the herd, utters a loud steam-whistle hiss. They all look up, raising their little heads on their long necks. Then they troop off, following their leader out across a shallow, rain-dappled river. The soil of the riverbank is trampled and churned underfoot. In millions of years' time, the rocks formed here will not have the crisp, well-defined layers that geologists would normally expect to find in rocks formed from river sediments. Instead, they will be all stirred up and mixed by the messy *Barosaurus* footprints – "bioturbation" is the fancy name that geologists give to this action.

As the *Barosaurus* cross the river, the youngsters huddle together for safety in the middle of the herd between the big adults. The nervousness of such huge beasts and the defensive structure of the herd remind us that this is actually a very dangerous place and time. There must be some pretty big meat-eaters around. We don't want to draw attention to ourselves, so we'd better tread carefully and try not to make too much noise.

Trouble!

Keeping an eye open for big theropods such as *Allosaurus*, or even medium-sized theropods like *Marshosaurus*, or small theropods such as *Ornitholestes*, we continue our exploration of the forest. But, just our luck, it is one of the big ones that spots us. An *Allosaurus* emerges from behind a tree and notices us the

DILOPHOSAURUS, OF THE EARLY JURASSIC, WAS ONE OF THE FIRST LARGE THEROPODS. THE CREST ON ITS HEAD WAS PROBABLY USED TO ATTRACT MATES.

ALLOSAURUS WAS ABOUT 11 M (36 FT)
LONG. IT PREFERRED TO AMBUSH PREY,
BUT WOULD GIVE CHASE IF
NECESSARY.

A welcome diversion

Suddenly we find ourselves in more open country. The forested areas are separated by large areas of more open ground. And there in front of us, swinging its tail leisurely and casting shadows with the broad, diamond-shaped plates on its back, stands a *Stegosaurus*. The plated plant-eater seems to prefer the more open spaces to the confined forests. Out in the open, its plates will not become entangled in branches and the wind can keep its enormous body cool.

The *Allosaurus* plunges out of the greenery behind us and halts abruptly, distracted by the plated dinosaur. We do not expect the *Stegosaurus* to run

very moment we notice it. Before long, its little brain registers that we are potential food. With a bellow it opens its wicked mouth and charges. Run! We take to our heels, dodging around tree-trunks to try to shake off our blood-thirsty pursuer. We start to panic as we realize just how fast this large animal can run – it's gaining on us!

away. Look at those hind legs. The thigh is longer than the shin. This is the sign of a slow-moving animal, because such a leg is not built for speed. It is an animal that will stand its ground. We expect a fight, but we are disappointed. The *Allosaurus* turns and stalks back into the greenery. It's more interested in picking off a young or sickly *Barosaurus* from the herd than staying here and tussling with the *Stegosaurus*.

That was a lucky escape for us. As the sun goes down over the Jurassic landscape, silhouetting a herd of *Brachiosaurus* against the fading light, we realize that this is no place for humans.

ALLOSAURUS WOULD SELDOM ATTACK AN ADULT BRACHIOSAURUS WEIGHING AROUND 70 TONNES, BUT ITS YOUNG WERE SOMETIMES A TARGET.

CRETACEOUS CROSSING

N ow we are white-water rafting in the highlands of late Cretaceous North America, about 70 million years ago. We can call places by modern names, because Pangaea has broken up into the individual continents, which are slowly drifting into their familiar positions.

R afting in the Rockies
The current carries us down the mountain river at breakneck speed. These mountains are the young Rockies, thrust up as the continent of North America pushes westwards against the floor of the

FLOWERING PLANTS BEGAN TO TAKE OVER FROM FERNS, HORSETAILS, AND CYCADS. THERE WERE MODERN-LOOKING CONIFERS AND BROAD-LEAVED TREES.

Pacific Ocean, wrinkling up the rocks along the edge as it goes. The rocks are sediments laid down in Triassic and Jurassic times – we can see fossils of *Coelophysis* footprints and ichthyosaur bones in the crags that rise around us. Up here in the windy heights there are few animals to be seen. The dark shapes of giant pterosaurs swoop around the cloudy peaks in the distance. These are pterodactyloids, the short-tailed type of pterosaur (the long-tailed types, the rhamphorhynchoids, have all died out by now). But the flying things in the mountain bushes nearby are all birds.

EUROPE
NORTH AMERICA
ASIA
AFRICA
INDIA
SOUTH AMERICA
AUSTRALIA
ANTARCTICA

AS THE CONTINENTS DRIFTED APART, THE WORLD STARTED TO TAKE ON A MORE FAMILIAR SHAPE TO MODERN EYES.

Mountain vegetation
The torrent carries us onwards, through the gorges, over rapids, and down towards the foothills. The current eases as we drift along. Stands of conifers with a ferny undergrowth line the banks.

AN ANKYLOSAUR'S WEAK SPOT WAS ITS SOFT, UNPROTECTED BELLY

STEGOCERAS WAS A DOME-HEADED DINOSAUR LIKE PACHYCEPHALOSAURUS. RIVAL MALES MAY HAVE SETTLED DISPUTES OVER FEMALES OR TERRITORY BY BUTTING ONE ANOTHER WITH THEIR DOMED SKULLS.

Beasts ahoy!
We round a corner and come across our first big animals. On the inside of the river bend, where some flat rocks form a partly submerged shelf, two dome-headed *Pachycephalosaurus* drink from the water. They are startled to see us and quickly disappear into the forest.

Where they vanished, a broad armoured back can be seen rising above the ferns. An ankylosaur of some kind pushes through the undergrowth, its head down as it feeds from the low-growing plants. As we pass by, we see that it is one of the side-spiked ankylosaurs, like *Edmontonia*. However, it is difficult to see the exact arrangement of armour, so we cannot be sure of its identity.

This all makes sense. The most common fossils from bone-headed dinosaurs are of the solid skulls, and these are usually badly worn as though

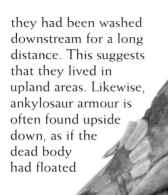

they had been washed downstream for a long distance. This suggests that they lived in upland areas. Likewise, ankylosaur armour is often found upside down, as if the dead body had floated

TO DEFEND ITSELF, EDMONTONIA WOULD CHARGE ATTACKERS AND STAB THEM WITH ITS SHARP SHOULDER AND FLANK SPIKES.

downstream and turned over as it decayed. This is the mountain life of the Cretaceous Period.

Modern plants

Now the vegetation begins to change. As we float farther downstream, the plant life becomes more colourful. The undergrowth now consists of little yellow flowers that resemble buttercups. Bushes with big blooms like magnolias line the banks. The primitive conifers of the higher slopes are now replaced by trees that look like willows and oaks. We could almost be looking at the vegetation of our own time, but something seems to be missing and we cannot tell what that is.

Plains migrants

Before long, the river leaves the forests of the hills and meanders over a lowland plain. Here the vegetation is of cycads and ferns – back to what it was like in Triassic and Jurassic times. *Pachyrhinosaurus* and other

MAGNOLIA IS A SURVIVOR FROM CRETACEOUS TIMES, WHEN FLOWERING SPECIES BECAME THE DOMINANT PLANT GROUP.

MIGRATING PACHYRHINOSAURUS MAY HAVE TRUDGED 50 KM (31 MILES) A DAY.

horned dinosaurs of the ceratopsian group live here. We spy herds of them following us down the stream. This does not surprise us – in our own time we have seen pictures of herds of plant-eating animals, such as buffalo or wildebeest, migrating across plains. Here the situation must be the same. The herds move from one area to another, depending on the season and where there is food to be had.

WEIRD WORLD
FOSSIL SAUROPOD BONES WERE ONCE USED AS BUILDING BRICKS. A CABIN IN COLORADO, USA, WAS BUILT FROM THESE FOSSILS BY A SHEPHERD, BEFORE ANYONE KNEW WHAT THE "BRICKS" REALLY WERE!

A watery grave

We notice well-trodden banks where the ceratopsian herds have been scrambling through mud to cross the river. There must be many disasters as herds are caught and washed away in flash floods. You can just imagine the panic and struggle as terrified animals trample and crush one another, and the crocodiles wait patiently for the losers.

In the distance, among some cycads, we can see the long necks of a couple of sauropods. Most of the sauropods have gone by now, being largely Jurassic beasts, but there are still a few left. And these seem to be restricted to the areas where the Jurassic-type vegetation of

A refuge

The current slows and plants close in around us. Instead of paddling down a broad river we are now drifting in a swamp. The river seems to have lost its course as it flows between the trunks of swamp trees and becomes choked with floating weed. Big shapes can be seen in the water here. A herd of duck-billed dinosaurs, *Edmontosaurus*, wallows in the shallows. These are not usually aquatic animals. They must be searching for food here, or else they are trying to get away from some danger. Danger it is! This is the home of one of the biggest meat-eaters of all time – the mighty *Tyrannosaurus*.

Dangerous country

The raft is aground. There is no more current. We will have to wade ashore if we want to see anything else. There's not far to go before we see what it was that frightened the herd of

SALTASAURUS, OF THE LATE CRETACEOUS, WAS RELATIVELY SMALL FOR A SAUROPOD. IT HAD BONY PLATES AND NODULES SET INTO THE SKIN OF ITS BACK.

IN MOST DISPUTES OVER FOOD, THE
WEAKER TYRANNOSAURUS WOULD BACK
OFF. BUT IF FOOD WAS
SCARCE, A FIERCE
FIGHT COULD
TAKE PLACE.

Edmontosaurus.
A big *Tyrannosaurus* is
crouched over the body
of a freshly killed
duck-bill, tearing it apart.
And as we watch, it is
joined by another
Tyrannosaurus.
A rival, or a mate?

Maybe not,
but let's take
the risk. We
lose sight of it
briefly, but suddenly
there is an eruption of
growls and hisses, and a
crashing of vegetation. It
seems to have got into a fight.

Close combat

The first meat-eater snarls and
growls at the newcomer, which
keeps approaching. Now the
first begins to gesture and
bellow. It is not going
to share its kill. The
newcomer gets the
message and, after a
few half-hearted
growls, it turns and
stalks away through
the forest. Would it
be wise to follow this
beast, to see where
it goes?

AND THEN THERE WERE NONE!

Meteorite impact
Maybe the extinction of the dinosaurs, 65 million years ago, was a sudden event. Imagine that you are watching the skies. In an instant, everything is engulfed in a dazzling light as a vast meteorite blasts through the atmosphere and explodes just behind the horizon. A few seconds later, the shock wave pounds you to pieces where you stand. That is sudden! If you are a few hundred kilometres away, the shock wave will take several minutes to reach you. If you are not killed instantly, you will be hammered by flying stones and branches. Red-hot fragments will rain down from the sky. Perhaps the impact of the meteorite throws up an enormous ocean wave that sweeps inland, destroying everything in its path.

WHAM! SHOCK WAVES RACE ACROSS THE GLOBE AS A GIANT METEORITE CRASHES INTO THE EARTH.

Even on the other side of the world you will not be safe. You may well survive the initial shock wave, feeling it like a distant earthquake, but dust, smoke, and steam thrown up into the atmosphere will prevent much of the Sun's light and heat from reaching the Earth's surface. Over the next few months, all the plants will die. You will have no food. It will become cold. You will freeze to death – that is, if you have not already died of starvation. This nightmare scenario is not just guesswork – there is evidence to support the idea that a meteorite may have ended the dinosaurs' reign.

E Evidence of the impact
In rocks that were laid down at the very end of the Cretaceous Period there are traces of the element iridium. This element is not often found at the Earth's surface, and the most likely source is from a meteorite.

RINGS OF MOUNTAINS WOULD HAVE MARKED THE IMPACT SITE FOR SEVERAL MILLION YEARS AFTERWARDS.

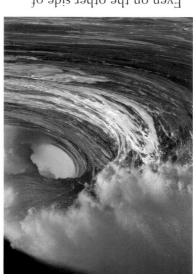

HUGE OCEAN WAVES MAY HAVE POUNDED THE LOW-LYING LANDS AFTER A METEORITE IMPACT, SWEEPING AWAY ALL LIFE.

There is also a buried structure that may be a vast meteorite crater in the Yucatán peninsula, Mexico, which dates from about the right time. What's more, beds of debris apparently laid down by giant waves have been found in rocks from the southern USA. All of this suggests that a meteorite the size of a small city struck the Earth in the Caribbean region about 65 million years ago.

Lots of lava

On the other hand, much of this damage could have been caused by volcanoes. Half of India is made up of lava flows that erupted about 65 million years ago. Volcanic eruptions as intense as this would have thrown up dust, smoke, and

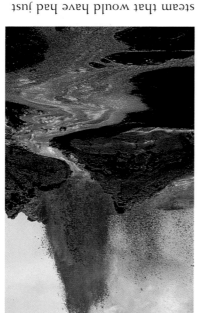

steam that would have had just the same effect on the climate as the debris from a meteorite impact. The element iridium is found in volcanic debris, as well as in meteorite rocks, so that might explain the high

VAST OUTPOURINGS OF LAVA ARE USUALLY ACCOMPANIED BY GAS AND STEAM CLOUDS THAT CAN ALTER THE CLIMATE.

EVEN THE BEST FOSSILIZED DINOSAURS, SUCH AS THIS EDMONTOSAURUS , TELL US NOTHING ABOUT WHAT WIPED THEM OUT.

levels of iridium in sediments laid down at that time.

Climate and disease

Meteorites? Volcanoes? All very dramatic. But maybe the dinosaurs' demise was not so spectacular. If, after millions of years of settled climates, the climates became colder or hotter, or wetter or drier, the dinosaurs might not have been able to cope with the changes, and gradually died out. Climate change may have happened if the sea level rose or fell, or if small landmasses merged to become bigger landmasses.

Perhaps disease was the big killer. You don't go to school if you have flu because

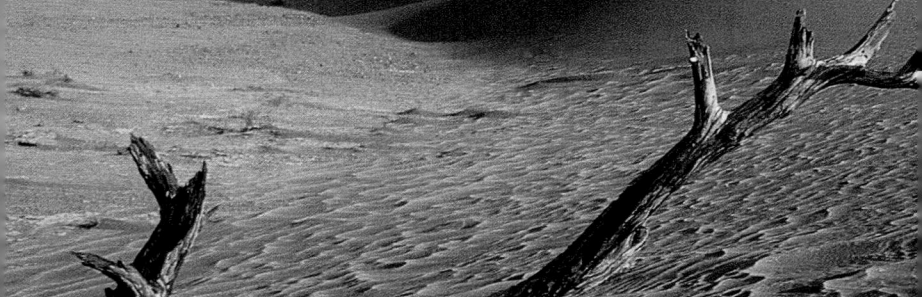

you don't want anybody else to catch it. But if everyone at school has already had the flu, you don't worry too much, because they will now be immune to it. Now imagine you are a dinosaur, and changing sea levels mean that you are able to migrate to new lands and meet other dinosaurs. You will spread diseases among them – diseases to which you are immune. And they will give you their diseases as well. Whole dinosaur communities may have been wiped out like this at the end of the Cretaceous Period.

A regular event

Whatever happened to wipe out the dinosaurs and the other animals of the time, it was not so unusual. Mass extinctions of this scale have happened about five times in the Earth's history. Smaller mass-extinctions are more frequent. Think of all the animals that have become extinct in the last few hundred years – the dodo, the passenger pigeon, and the Tasmanian wolf, to name just a few. It is possible that we are living through a mass-extinction at the moment. Worrying, isn't it?

GREAT CLIMATE CHANGES – SUCH AS THE EARTH BECOMING HOTTER AND DRIER – MAY HAVE CAUSED THE DINOSAURS' DECLINE.

WEIRD WORLD
IF THE DINOSAURS HAD NOT BECOME EXTINCT, WE WOULD NOT BE HERE NOW. IT WAS THE DINOSAURS' DISAPPEARANCE THAT ALLOWED THE MAMMALS TO BECOME THE DOMINANT ANIMALS ON EARTH.

THE DINOSAUR'S CHANGING FACE

The first dinosaur pictures and models looked very different from the ones we see today. We may be tempted to laugh at these early efforts, but they weren't bad considering that dinosaur pioneers had just a few bones and teeth to go on. The rest had to be clever guesswork.

The first restoration

If somebody gave you, say, an eye and a toenail and asked you to draw the animal that they came from, you could draw a very strange beast indeed, or you could draw something that you knew. This is pretty much how the first discoverers of dinosaur remains had to work.

In the 1820s, Dr Gideon Mantell and his wife Mary discovered fossilized bones and teeth in the Cretaceous rocks of Sussex, in southern England. Mantell was a country doctor who studied fossils as a hobby. He knew that these were reptile bones, and the teeth were like giant versions of those found in the modern plant-eating iguana lizard. That was all he knew. It is hardly surprising then that his restoration looked like a giant iguana. And that is why he named the animal *Iguanodon*, meaning "iguana-toothed".

A name for the giant reptiles

Sir Richard Owen, the most famous British naturalist of his day, invented the name "dinosaur" in 1841. At that time, there had been only three dinosaurs found – the ornithopod *Iguanodon*,

AN IGUANA LIZARD – LIKENED TO A DINOSAUR BY EARLY PALAEONTOLOGISTS.

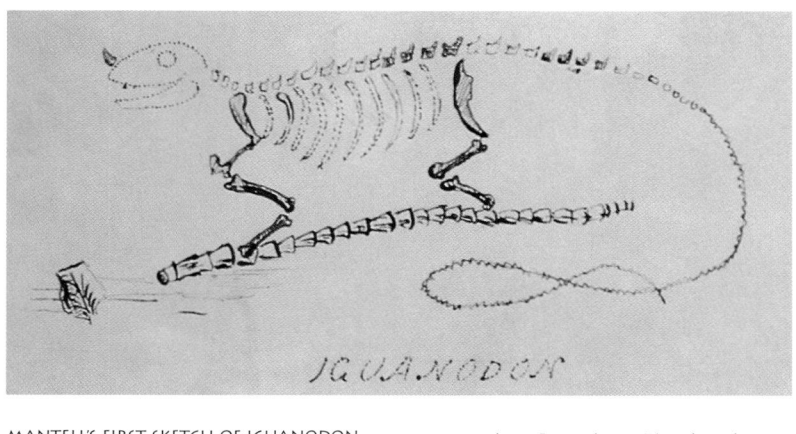

MANTELL'S FIRST SKETCH OF IGUANODON SHOWS A FOUR-FOOTED LIZARD.

the theropod *Megalosaurus*, and the ankylosaur *Hylaeosaurus*. (We still do not know a lot about that last one.) Soon it became like it is today – everyone was fascinated by dinosaurs and wanted to know more. When the Crystal Palace park was opened in London, England, in 1853, parts of the grounds were turned into the first dinosaur theme park. Concrete statues of all the dinosaurs known were set up, along with statues of the sea reptiles and pterosaurs. They are still there today – totally inaccurate, but beautifully

THE CRYSTAL PALACE STATUES REFLECT WONDERFULLY THE 19TH-CENTURY KNOWLEDGE OF DINOSAURS.

IF WE ONLY HAD THE SKULL OF A RABBIT TO GO ON, WE WOULDN'T BE ABLE TO TELL THAT WHEN IT WAS ALIVE IT HAD CHUBBY CHEEKS, LONG EARS, AND FUR.

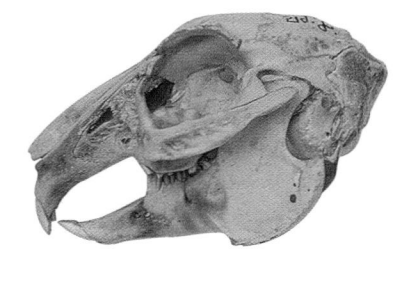

atmospheric and excellent for understanding the state of knowledge at the time.

New discoveries

The first American finds were made in the 1850s, the best of which was the partial skeleton of a duck-billed *Hadrosaurus* found in New Jersey and described by Joseph Leidy, a professor of anatomy. The skeleton showed an animal whose hind legs were longer than its front ones, suggesting that it walked on two legs.

Then came an even better discovery. Over 30 *Iguanodon* skeletons were found in a Belgian mine in 1878, and most of those were complete and still joined together. Now people were getting a better idea of what dinosaurs were like.

Images based on evidence

A restoration is only as good as the evidence available. Imagine you had been given a pile of, let's say, rabbit skeletons, and most of those were still joined together. If you had never seen a rabbit and you were asked to draw a restoration of one based only on those skeletons, what would

A MODERN RECONSTRUCTION OF AN IGUANODON SHOWS AN ANIMAL WITH A HORIZONTAL BACKBONE. IT PROBABLY SPENT MOST OF ITS TIME ON ALL FOURS.

the result be? Probably you would not give it the rounded, furry cheeks that hide the big gnawing teeth. Certainly you would not know that it was supposed to have long ears. And what about the white cottontail? The picture you drew would be closer to a real rabbit than one

America, ornithopods such as *Iguanodon* and *Hadrosaurus* were shown as upright animals. And that is how things stayed for nearly 100 years.

I guanodon today

By the mid-20th century, scientists had learned more

MANY DINOSAURS ARE KNOWN FROM A SINGLE BONE

drawn from just an eye and a toenail, but it would still not be accurate. Based on the Belgian skeletons and the finds from

about how animals are built and the way that they interact with their environment. They could also apply engineering principles to dinosaur skeletons to show how

THIS EARLY RECONSTRUCTION OF IGUANODON SHOWED AN UPRIGHT ANIMAL SITTING ON ITS TAIL LIKE A KANGAROO.

they moved. Large ornithopods were now restored as four-footed animals that held their tails clear of the ground. They only rose on their hind legs now and again, but probably skittered around two-footedly as youngsters. Nowadays

we can build what we are sure is a pretty accurate model of an *Iguanodon*. Look at the picture below. Yes, you've sussed it –

we've been using models throughout this book. We are luckier than Dr Mantell, nearly 200 years ago. We not only have a lot more knowledge about the lives and habits of animals of the past, but we can also use science and imagination to reconstruct the amazing world of the dinosaurs.

THIS RESTORATION OF IGUANODON MAY CHANGE AS NEW DISCOVERIES ARE MADE.

WEIRD WORLD
TO CELEBRATE THE COMPLETION OF THE CRYSTAL PALACE DINOSAURS, A SPECIAL NEW YEAR'S EVE DINNER WAS HELD – INSIDE THE HOLLOW CONCRETE MODEL OF IGUANODON!

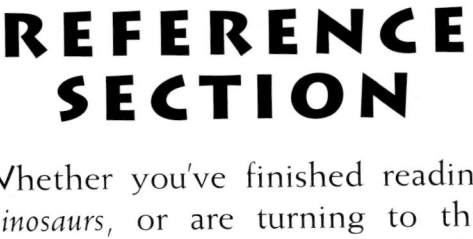

REFERENCE SECTION

Whether you've finished reading *Dinosaurs*, or are turning to this section first, you'll find the information on the next eight pages really useful. Here are all the facts and figures, background details, meanings of dinosaur names, and unfamiliar words that you might need. There's also a list of website addresses – so, whether you want to surf the net or search out facts, these pages should turn you from an enthusiast into an expert.

DINOSAURS IN THIS BOOK

NAME OF DINOSAUR	MEANING OF NAME	WHEN IT LIVED (period/millions of years ago)	
Ankylosaurs			
Ankylosaurus	Stiff lizard	Cretaceous	70 mya
Edmontonia	From Edmonton	Cretaceous	73 mya
Euoplocephalus	Well-shielded head	Cretaceous	73 mya
Hylaeosaurus	Forest lizard	Cretaceous	125 mya
Nodosaurus	Knobbed lizard	Cretaceous	105 mya
Ceratopsians			
Pachyrhinosaurus	Thick nosed lizard	Cretaceous	70 mya
Protoceratops	First horned face	Cretaceous	80 mya
Psittacosaurus	Parrot lizard	Cretaceous	100 mya
Styracosaurus	Spear-spike lizard	Cretaceous	75 mya
Torosaurus	Perforated lizard	Cretaceous	68 mya
Triceratops	Three horned face	Cretaceous	66 mya
Ornithopods			
Brachylophosaurus	Short-crested lizard	Cretaceous	75 mya
Corythosaurus	Helmet lizard	Cretaceous	74 mya
Edmontosaurus	Lizard of Edmonton	Cretaceous	70 mya
Hadrosaurus	Sturdy lizard	Cretaceous	75 mya
Hypsilophodon	High-ridged tooth	Cretaceous	120 mya
Iguanodon	Iguana tooth	Cretaceous	120 mya
Maiasaura	Good mother lizard	Cretaceous	75 mya
Pachycephalosaurs			
Pachycephalosaurus	Thick headed lizard	Cretaceous	66 mya
Stegoceras	Roof horn	Jurassic	70 mya
Prosauropods			
Ammosaurus	Sand lizard	Jurassic	190 mya
Plateosaurus	Broad lizard	Triassic	220 mya

TIMELINE OF PERIODS AND ERAS

286 MILLION YEARS AGO	245 MILLION YEARS AGO	208 MILLION YEARS AGO
Permian Period	**Triassic Period**	**Jurassic Period**
Palaeozoic Era	Mesozoic Era	

Sauropods

Apatosaurus	Deceptive lizard	Jurassic	150 mya
Argentinosaurus	Lizard of Argentina	Cretaceous	93 mya
Barosaurus	Heavy lizard	Jurassic	150 mya
Brachiosaurus	Arm lizard	Jurassic	150 mya
Diplodocus	Double beam	Jurassic	150 mya
Hypselosaurus	High lizard	Cretaceous	71 mya
Saltasaurus	Salta lizard	Cretaceous	80 mya
Sauroposeidon	Poseidon's lizard	Cretaceous	115 mya
Seismosaurus	Earth-shaking lizard	Jurassic	150 mya

Stegosaurs

Kentrosaurus	Spiked lizard	Jurassic	152 mya
Stegosaurus	Roofed lizard	Jurassic	150 mya

Theropods

Albertosaurus	Lizard of Alberta	Cretaceous	72 mya
Allosaurus	Strange lizard	Jurassic	150 mya
Bambiraptor	Baby robber	Cretaceous	75 mya
Baryonyx	Heavy claw	Cretaceous	125 mya
Carnotaurus	Meat-eating bull	Cretaceous	100 mya
Coelophysis	Hollow form	Triassic	215 mya
Compsognathus	Pretty jaw	Jurassic	150 mya
Deinonychus	Terrible claw	Cretaceous	113 mya
Dilophosaurus	Double-crested lizard	Triassic	200 mya
Eoraptor	Dawn robber	Triassic	228 mya
Gallimimus	Chicken mimic	Cretaceous	73 mya
Giganotosaurus	Giant southern lizard	Cretaceous	83 mya
Herrerasaurus	Herrera's lizard	Triassic	228 mya
Marshosaurus	Marsh's lizard	Jurassic	150 mya
Megalosaurus	Big lizard	Jurassic,	165 mya
Ornitholestes	Bird stealer	Jurassic	150 mya
Ornithomimus	Bird mimic	Cretaceous	70 mya
Oviraptor	Egg robber	Cretaceous	80 mya
Suchomimus	Crocodile mimic	Cretaceous	120 mya
Troodon	Tearing tooth	Cretaceous	68 mya
Tyrannosaurus	Tyrant lizard	Cretaceous	65 mya
Utahraptor	Utah robber	Cretaceous	125 mya
Velociraptor	Fast robber	Cretaceous	80 mya

146 MILLION YEARS AGO	65 MILLION YEARS AGO	NOW
Cretaceous Period	**Tertiary & Quaternary Periods**	
Mesozoic Era	Cenozoic Era	

MILESTONES OF DISCOVERY

1822 James Parkinson, a doctor, gives the name *Megalosaurus* to a jawbone found in Oxfordshire, England

1824 Dean William Buckland, a clergyman, publishes a scientific description of *Megalosaurus* – the first serious study of a dinosaur.

1825 Dr. Gideon Mantell publishes a description of *Iguanodon*.

1837 Palaeontologist Hermann von Meyer publishes a description of *Plateosaurus*.

1842 Naturalist Sir Richard Owen invents the name "Dinosauria", later shortened to dinosaur.

1854 Life-sized dinosaur statues unveiled at Crystal Palace in London.

1856 Anatomist Joseph Leidy publishes a description of *Hadrosaurus*, the first North American discovery.

1859 The publication of Charles Darwin's book *The Origin of Species* puts the dinosaurs' development into an evolutionary context.

1860 First discovery of dinosaur-bird *Archaeopteryx* in Germany.

1870s & 1880s In the USA, fossil hunters Othniel Marsh and Edward Cope compete with one another for the best fossil discoveries. This bitter dispute becomes known as the "bone wars". About 150 new dinosaurs are discovered during this period.

1874 George Dawson discovers the first Canadian dinosaur.

1878 Over 30 *Iguanodon* skeletons are found in Belgium, giving a good idea of how dinosaurs were built.

1887 Palaeontologist Henry Seeley sets up the lizard-hip/bird-hip classification system.

1907–12 German expeditions unearth the first dinosaur skeletons in Africa.

1910–17 American and Canadian teams vie to find the best remains in Canada in a fossil "gold rush".

1922 American expeditions in the Gobi Desert led by Roy Chapman Andrews find the first undisputed dinosaur eggs in the Gobi desert.

1930s China is found to have many excellent dinosaur remains.

1938 Serious study of dinosaur footprints begins with R. T. Bird's discovery of fossil tracks in Texas.

1944 Allied bombing destroys valuable African specimens in Berlin, Germany, and also a dinosaur theme park, Hagenbeck's, in Hamburg.

1970s South America is found to be rich in dinosaur remains.

1969 John Ostrom suggests that dinosaurs were warm-blooded and gave rise to birds.

1974 Robert Bakker and Peter Galton argue that birds are dinosaurs.

1980 Dinosaur "bonebeds" are found in Canada, showing the mass death of a herd of horned dinosaurs.

1980 Luis and Walter Alvarez suggest that dinosaur extinction was due to a meteorite impact.

1980s Significant dinosaur discoveries are made in Australia.

1986 The first dinosaur discovery (an ankylosaur) is made in Antarctica.

1990s American expeditions to Madagascar find many important dinosaur remains.

1996 The first of many feathered dinosaurs is found in China.

DINOSAUR FAMILY TREE

JURASSIC	TRIASSIC	CRETACEOUS

Stegosaurs

Ankylosaurs

Ornithopods

Pachycephalosaurs

Ceratopsians

Bird-hips

Lizard-hips

Prosauropods

Sauropods

Ceratosaurs (Dilophosaurs, etc.)

Dromaeosaurs (Raptors)

Theropods

Birds

Tyrannosaurs

Primitive types
(Herrerosaurs, etc.)

Allosaurs

Spinosaurs (*Baryonyx*, etc.)

DINOSAUR WEBSITES

http://kids.discovery.com/fansites/prehistoric/prehistoric.html
Hear dino sounds, watch how dinos move, and build a dino from bones.

www.isgs.uiuc.edu/dinos/dinos_home.html
Lot of excellent dino links at Dino Russ's Lair.

http://Ology.amnh.org/paleontology/index.html
Read interviews with dinosaurs, use an interactive dino family tree, and follow palaeontologists into the Gobi Desert on a fossil hunt.

www.nationalgeographic.com/features/96/dinoeggs/
Learn about dino mothers and babies, and hunt eggs with the experts.

DINO RECORDS

Longest dinosaur known
Seismosaurus, perhaps 50 m (164 ft).
Heaviest dinosaur known
Argentinosaurus, perhaps 100 tonnes.
Biggest predator
Giganotosaurus, perhaps 12.5 m
(41 ft) long and weighing 8 tonnes.
Smallest complete dinosaur known
Compsognathus, about 1 m (40 in) long.
Most intelligent dinosaur known
Troodon, with the largest
brain-to-body size

Dumbest dinosaur known
Apatosaurus, with the smallest brain-
to-body size
Fastest runner
Gallimimus, about 80 kmh (50 mph).
First dinosaur in space
Coelophysis – a fossil was taken up in
the Space Shuttle in 1998!
**[These figures only refer to the
dinosaurs we know, and we think
that we know only about one-fifth
of the dinosaurs that existed.]**

SCIENTIFIC STUDIES

**The two main sciences involved
in the study of dinosaurs are
geology (the study of the earth)
and biology (the study of life).
Within these sciences are all
manner of other studies…**

Palaeontology   The study of
ancient life. Under this banner come
various studies, such as invertebrate
palaeontology and vertebrate
palaeontology, and also some
of the following terms.
Palaeozoology   The study
of ancient animal life.
Palaeobotany   The study
of ancient plant life.
Ichnology   The study of footprints
and other trace fossils
Taphonomy   The study of what
happens to dead organisms before
they become fossilized.
Stratigraphy   The study of the

layers of sedimentary rocks, the
sequence in which they were laid
down, and the conditions under
which they formed.
Palaeogeography   The study of the
ancient landforms – the positions of
the continents, the climates, and the
environmental conditions at different
periods of geological time.
Systematics   The study of the
diversity of organisms and their
relationships to one another.
Taxonomy   The practice of naming
different organisms on the basis of
their relationships.
Biogeography   The study of what
animals and plants are found in
different places, and why they
occur there.
Sedimentology   The study of
the formation of sediments and
sedimentary rocks, in which fossils
are found.

DINOSAUR GLOSSARY

Ammonite
A Mesozoic marine animal, like an octopus with a coiled shell.

Amphibian
Any vertebrate animal that spends its early stage in the water but its adult stage on land. Frogs, with their tadpoles, are modern amphibians.

Ankylosaur
An armoured, bird-hipped dinosaur.

Bed
A layer of sedimentary rock.

Belemnite
A Mesozoic marine animal, like a squid but with a hard, pencil-like shell.

Ceratopsian
A horned, bird-hipped dinosaur.

Coal
An organic sedimentary rock made up of fragments of plant material.

Conifer
A seed-bearing tree that reproduces by means of cones.

Coprolite
A fossilized animal dropping.

Cretaceous
The period of time lasting from 146 to 65 million years ago. The last of the three periods in the Mesozoic era.

Cycad
A primitive seed-bearing plant. Cycads look like palm trees, but are more closely related to conifers.

Diagenesis
The process by which sediments turn into sedimentary rock.

Duck-bill
A bird-hipped dinosaur with a duck-like beak.

Environment
The surroundings of an animal or plant – including the climate, the landscape, the altitude, the other animals, and the plants living there.

Erosion
The natural process whereby exposed rocks are broken down and worn away.

Flash flood
A sudden flood that sweeps down a river, following heavy rain upstream.

Fossil
The remains of a once-living thing preserved in rock.

Gastrolith
A stone swallowed by an animal to help in its digestion. In swimming animals, such as crocodiles, stones may be swallowed and used to adjust buoyancy.

Ginkgo
A type of tree with fan-shaped leaves.

Glass fibre
A tough building material consisting of hairs of glass embedded in resin.

Gizzard
Part of the digestive system of a bird, and some dinosaurs, that holds stones (gastroliths) used for grinding up food.

Horsetail
A primitive plant, related to ferns, that consists of a vertical stem with regular whorls of leaves.

Ichnology
The study of footprints.

Ichthyosaur
A fish-shaped marine reptile common in the Mesozoic Era.

Iguana
A modern-day plant-eating lizard from South and Central America.

Immune
Resistant to infection, unable to catch a disease.

Intestines
Tubes in the body through which food passes, and which absorb nutrients.

Invertebrate
An animal without a backbone.

Jurassic Period
The second period of the Mesozoic Era. The Jurassic lasted from 208 to 146 million years ago.

Laboratory
A place where scientific work is done.

Mace
A club-like ancient weapon that consisted of a heavy head at the end of a rigid shaft.

Mammal
A type of hairy, warm-blooded, vertebrate animal whose females produce milk and suckle their young. Humans are mammals.

Marsupial
A type of mammal whose females carry their young in a pouch on the body.

Mass-extinction
An event during which many different types of animal and plant die out.

Mesozoic
The era of history stretching from 245 to 65 million years ago and comprising the Triassic, Jurassic, and Cretaceous periods. The era preceding the Mesozoic was the Palaeozoic, when life began to move from the sea to the land. (All time before the Palaeozoic, when only very simple life existed, is called Precambrian.) The era following the Mesozoic was the Cenozoic, which includes the Age of Mammals and brings us up to the present day.

Meteorite
A piece of rock that has fallen to Earth from space.

Migrate
To travel from one area to another, usually in response to changing living conditions such as climate or the availability of food.

Mineral
An inorganic substance that is formed naturally by geological processes. Rocks are accumulations of minerals.

Mosasaur
A sea-living reptile from the Cretaceous period, closely related to modern monitor lizards.

Muscle
Elastic body tissue that produces movement.

Organic
Derived from or relating to living things.

Organism
A living thing.

Ornithopod
A bird-hipped, plant-eating dinosaur with feet like those of a bird.

Pachycephalosaur
A bird-hipped dinosaur with a very thick skull.

Palaeontologist
A scientist who uses fossil remains to study ancient animal and plant life.

Pangaea
The single supercontinent that existed during the Triassic period. It consisted of all the continents of the world fused together.

Panthalassa
The vast Triassic ocean that covered the part of the world not occupied by Pangaea.

Plesiosaur
A Mesozoic marine reptile with

either a long neck or a long head, and paddle-shaped limbs.

Predator
An animal that actively hunts other animals, known as prey, for food.

Preparator
A technician skilled in removing fossils from rock so that they can be studied by palaeontologists.

Prosauropod
A lizard-hipped dinosaur that existed in the Triassic and early Jurassic periods. It resembled a primitive type of sauropod.

Pterosaur
A flying reptile of the Mesozoic Era.

Pubis
One of the bones of the hip. In dinosaurs it either stuck forwards or was swept back. The classification of dinosaurs into bird- and lizard-hipped dinosaurs is based on the position of the pubis. In lizard-hipped dinosaurs the pubis pointed forwards, while in bird-hipped dinosaurs it pointed backwards.

Raptor
Strictly speaking, a bird of prey like an eagle or a falcon, but the word raptor has now become a popular term for a member of the group of theropod dinosaurs that had a killing claw on the hind foot.

Reconstruction
A skeleton of an extinct animal, built up from fossilized bones or casts made from the bones.

Restoration
A picture, film animation, or sculpture that shows how an extinct animal such as a dinosaur would have looked when it was alive.

Sandstone
A sedimentary rock made up of sand

grains squashed together and then cemented by mineral deposits.

Sauropod
A lizard-hipped dinosaur. Sauropods were huge plant-eaters that had long necks and walked on all-fours.

Scavenger
An animal that feeds from the bodies of animals that are already dead.

Sediment
Material, such as sand, mud, or silt, that is deposited on the bed of a river or the ocean. When this undergoes diagenesis it turns into sedimentary rock.

Shingle
Rounded stones that are deposited on a shoreline by waves and currents.

Stegosaur
A bird-hipped dinosaur with plates and spines on its back.

Supercontinent
A vast continent that consists of several continental landmasses fused together.

Taphonomy
The study of dead organisms before they become fossilized.

Tendon
The strap-like tissue that attaches muscle to bones.

Theropod
A two-footed, lizard-hipped dinosaur that had strong hind legs, long jaws, and sharp teeth. All meat-eating dinosaurs were theropods.

Triassic Period
The first period of the Mesozoic Era, from 245 to 208 million years ago.

Vertebrate
An animal that has a backbone. The backbone, or spine, is made up of many individual bones, each one of which is called a vertebra.

INDEX

CREDITS

Dorling Kindersley would like to thank:

Nomazwe Mandonko and Almudena Diaz for DTP assistance, Kate Humby for proof-reading, and Chris Bernstein for compiling the index.

Additional photography by: Dave King, Andy Crawford, John Downes, Steve Gorton, Lynton Gardiner, Colin Keates, Harry Taylor, Jen and Des Bartlett and Gary Ombler.

Models made by: Roby Braun, Jonathan Hateley, and Gary Staab.